SITT
718 375 9547

THE
BOSTONER

THE
BOSTONER

*Stories and recollections
from the colorful Chassidic Court
of the Bostoner Rebbe,
Rabbi Levi I. Horowitz*

by

Hanoch Teller

FELDHEIM PUBLISHERS   Jerusalem • New York

The stories in this book are all true in essence, although certain pertinent details and the names of various private individuals have been altered so as to conceal the identity of those involved. Any similarity in these fictitious names to those of actual persons, living or dead, is purely coincidental.

A glossary of foreign words and phrases used in the text appears at the end of this book.

First published 1990

Copyright © 1990 by Hanoch Teller and Feldheim Publishers

Edited by Marsi Tabak

Library of Congress Cataloging-in-Publication Data

Teller, Hanoch.
    The Bostoner: Stories and recollections from the colorful Chassidic Court of The Bostoner Rebbe / by Hanoch Teller.
    208 p. 21.5 cm.
    ISBN 0-87306-507-7
    1. Horovits, Levi Yitsḥak, ha-Levi—Anecdotes. 2. Rabbis—Massachusetts —Boston—Anecdotes. 3. Hasidim—Massachusetts—Boston—Anecdotes. 4. Boston (Mass.)—Anecdotes. I. Horovits, Levi Yitsḥak, ha-Levi. II. Title.
    BM755.H66T45 1989
    296.8'332'092—dc20
    [B]   89-28325
            CIP

Philipp Feldheim Inc.
200 Airport Executive Park   Feldheim Publishers Ltd.
Spring Valley, NY 10977   POB 6525/Jerusalem, Israel

Printed in Israel   10 9 8 7 6 5 4 3 2 1

Also by
HANOCH TELLER

Once Upon A Soul

Soul Survivors

'Souled!'

The Steipler Gaon

Sunset

Courtrooms of the Mind

Above the Bottom Line

Pichifkes

Bridges of Steel, Ladders of Gold

Contents

Foreword by the Bostoner Rebbe, *shlita*

הרב לוי יצחק הלוי הורוויץ
בן הרה"צ ר' פינחס דוד זצוקי"ל — דער באסטאנער רבי

GRAND RABBI LEVI I. HOROWITZ

CONGREGATION BETH PINCHAS

1710 BEACON STREET
BROOKLINE 46, MASS.
REGENT 4-5100

ב"ה

Chassidic homes have always thrived on stories. In fact, it was through the spoken word that chassidic thought first spread. Shivchei HaBesh"t -- the very first chassidic sefer -- was a compilation of incidents that occurred during the lifetime of my forebear, the holy Baal Shem Tov, founder of chassidism. One of the foremost principles of chassidic philosophy is that Divine Providence applies to even the most chance of happenings. In this sense, every person's life story -- his sefer toldos adam -- is a lessonbook from which to see Hashgachah Pratis.

This volume records some of the incidents which Hashem placed in the path of the Chassidic Center during the course of four decades of communal service in America. The stories included here contain spiritual and universal lessons. Some deal with the guiding hand of the Almighty, and others emphasize the importance of mitzvah observance; some portray the power of trust in the Lord (bitachon), while others shed light on the true meaning of kindness (chessed).

I wholeheartedly endorse this book and hope that it will serve to educate and inspire many of our brethren. May Hashem grant that it accomplish its noble purpose.

I thank Hanoch Teller, the gifted and resourceful author and long-time friend of Boston, for his skillful rendering of the material. Fortunate are we that so talented a writer was selected to record these reminiscences. Rabbi Teller's distinctive style, sensitivity and humor are apparent on every page.

All the stories in this volume are true in essence, although expository license was taken in order to enhance the impact of the Torah lessons they convey. The book opens with two stories of my father and mentor, the first Bostoner Rebbe, Harav Pinchos Dovid Horowitz, zt"l, whose exemplary conduct and achievements I and all his followers have always striven to emulate. These are but a small sample of the rich heritage which Bostoner chassidus was so fortunate to inherit.

If this book will encourage its readers to reach out and touch the lives of others, dayenu. If it will help enable individuals to author their own sefer toldos adam, then I will feel especially gratified.

Preface

To most people who are neither New Englanders nor Red Sox fans, "Boston" usually brings to mind a Revolutionary tea party, a rich cream pie, or Harvard Yard. In more recent years, the thundering hoofbeats of Bostonian Paul Revere's noble steed were muted by the rifle reports that ended the life of Boston's most famous son, John Fitzgerald Kennedy. But for Jews the world over, Boston has an altogether different association: it is the home of the Bostoner Rebbe and the cradle of Bostoner *chassidus*.

As a young teen I was drawn to Boston not to view historic landmarks, but to attend *shiurim*. Having at the time neither family nor friends in Brookline — the Orthodox Jewish section of the city — I sought temporary lodging, and this brought me, like so many before and after me, to the door of the Bostoner Rebbe. The Rebbe and the Rebbetzin welcomed me into their home and into the world of *chassidus*.

How many unique Shabbos meals of the Rebbetzin's home-made gefilte fish, golden chicken soup and pungent cholent I consumed at the Rebbe's table I cannot remember, but I shall never forget the atmosphere, the words of Torah and the fascinating company. I was therefore especially complimented when I was approached to render the colorful incidents of the Bostoner court into book form.

As in all my previous works, I have, on the advice of my mentors, employed fictitious names throughout this book and altered various salient details so as to conceal identities and insure the privacy of the individuals concerned, except in the case of famous personalities (e.g., President Kennedy, Dr. Castanada). If in so doing, I have, Heaven forbid, offended anyone, it was wholly inadvertent.

In preparing the manuscript it was a privilege once again to be in close contact with the Rebbe's family and *chassidim* and I have benefited enormously from the experience. This book has also provided the opportunity for me to again work with my earlier collaborator and literary mentor, Marsi Tabak. Jascha Heifetz, the famous violinist, once commented that if he did not practice his art for one day, he could tell the difference; if he did not practice for two days, the *violin* could tell the difference; if he did not practice for three days, the *audience* could tell the difference. I know that I, and I'm sure the readers, can tell the difference when Marsi is or is not involved in my writing. The result of her involvement is harmonious music.

I doff my hat to Pesh Fischer, the kind and gracious navigator of the tortuous road maps we produced. I likewise extend my gratitude to Rabbi Ben Zion Sobel, Dr. Henry Romberg and Harvey Klineman for their highly professional contributions to this project.

I look forward to every book I write if only for the opportunity to publicly acknowledge the kindness and patience of my dear parents. But, alas, I realize that even this falls pitifully short of repayment for the debt of gratitude I owe. The same holds true when it comes to my wife. Bostoner *chassidus*, which is rooted in caring for others, could not hope to find a more enthusiastic *chassidusta*.

While on the lecture circuit, far from home, I have merited encountering such amiable pinch-hitters as Rabbi and Mrs. Dov Goldbaum and the Paskeszes, world renowned as the *sweetest* people in town, who provided me with a home-away-from-home.

I have also been blessed with the selfless assistance and inspiring guidance of the esteemed Rabbi Yitzchak and Bernice Ginsberg.

These trips would not be possible without the encouragement of Rabbi Jay Marcus, the extraordinarily receptive audiences wherever I travel, and the man who coordinates them for me, Rabbi Yitzchok Rosenberg. Thank you, thank you, thank you!

I pray this volume will draw widespread attention to the phenomenal accomplishments of Bostoner *chassidus*. Personally, I doubt that I would qualify as a Bostoner *chassid*, but I am certainly a *chassid* of the Bostoner Rebbe.

Hanoch Teller
Jerusalem, Elul 5749

Introduction

In the early 1900s, Reb Pinchos Dovid Horowitz was advised by his uncle, the noted Lelover Rebbe of Jerusalem (fondly known as Reb Dovid'l), to journey to America. Reb Pinchos was appalled at the thought of leaving the Holy Land for what was reputed to be a "*treife medina*" — a land devoid of sanctity. Jerusalem was his home.

Loath to heed his sagacious uncle's advice, he tarried in *Eretz Yisrael* until a major *din Torah* involving Jerusalem's residents was about to be adjudicated in Europe. The young scholar was dispatched abroad to represent his fellow Jerusalemites.

With most of Europe in the throes of war, the trip was fraught with danger. During his return voyage, Reb Pinchos, who was traveling on an Austrian passport, was apprehended by hostile authorities in Salonika, Greece and nearly incarcerated. The Chief Rabbi of Salonika,* alerted to the dilemma, helped him obtain a visa to one of the few countries that was still neutral... America!

Chassidim in Boston, Massachusetts beseeched Reb Pinchos to become their Rebbe, and the young *talmid chacham* complied. Thus began the Boston chassidic dynasty.

In the year 1916, Reb Pinchos established the first chassidic court (*cloiz*) in the "New World" which was open to one and all and greatly appreciated by Jews of every stripe.

* Later Chief Sephardi Rabbi of Palestine, Rabbi Yaakov Meir.

Concomitantly, he established a *beis midrash* in Boston and although he and his wife both had illustrious forebears, including the Yehudi of Pszyscha, the Seer of Lublin, the Maggid of Mezritch and the Baal Shem Tov, and he was a direct descendant of the courts of Lelov and Nikolsburg, Reb Pinchos chose for himself the simple designation of "the Bostoner," and this was how he was always known. He felt it would be misleading to those who might seek his counsel if he were known as the Lubliner or the Lelover Rebbe. "What can you expect from a *Bostoner* Rebbe?" he would inquire ironically.

Readers of this volume will form their own response to this query, but I suspect and hope that it will differ substantially from the answer which the original Bostoner Rebbe, in his humility, anticipated.

In 1940, after serving the Jewish community of Boston for twenty-five years, Reb Pinchos Dovid relocated to the Williamsburg section of Brooklyn. Very many European wayfarers had passed through Boston during that period and he had encouraged them to bring their families to America before they were caught up in the conflagration. Those who followed his advice found refuge in Williamsburg and they pressed the Rebbe to set up his court there. From the moment he arrived he initiated a rigorous campaign to lay down consistent public standards of religious observance.

Even after leaving Boston, however, the Rebbe did not sever his ties with that city. After living in New York for well over a year, he turned to his Rebbetzin one day and asked, "What is being done for Sue Eisenstein of Boston?" referring to a spinster who fervently wished to marry but who had not yet found her match. Silence was the only response the Rebbe received. Reb Pinchos Dovid seized the opportunity to express his dissatisfaction and, at the same time, convey a vital lesson. He turned to address his entire family and said, "The fact that a person is not facing you does not excuse you from extending yourself on his or her behalf." To underscore his point he related a story about the great *ohev Yisrael*, Reb Moshe Leib of Sassov, a story which embodied the entire thrust of Bostoner *chassidus*:

Reb Moshe Leib loved his fellow Jews and would reach out to them wherever they might be. He made frequent trips and daily excursions searching for lost souls, and one such pilgrimage brought him to a tavern. Undaunted by the surroundings, the Sassover Rebbe entered and witnessed a dramatic exchange between two Cossacks who were well into their cups.

"Igor," cried the Russian horseman to his comrade, "I love you!"

"No, you don't," Igor rebutted.

"But I do!" Ivan protested. "I love you more than anything in the world!"

Igor shook his head, denying the claim.

Ivan gulped down his vodka and tears burned his cheeks. "I swear to you, Igor, by the life of the Czar himself, there is nothing or no one that I love more than you!"

Igor arose from the bar and castigated his comrade. "If you really loved me, if you really and truly cared for me, then you would know what pains me and what I am lacking."

The Rebbe of Sassov walked out of the tavern sobered

and inspired by what he'd heard. "Unless I feel my brother's pain," he told himself, "and know what his unmet needs are, then I have failed in truly loving him."

Reb Moshe Leib's conclusion is the fulcrum of Bostoner *chassidus*: giving and caring for the needs of others. That ideal, embodied in the first Rebbe, was the legacy he bequeathed to his sons, Reb Moshe and Reb Levi Yitzchak, who grew up in a home where Reb Moshe Leib's credo was practiced daily.

The venerable Reb Pinchos Dovid, in poor health and nearly blind for the last twenty years of his life, never faltered in his love of his fellow Jew. His home was a haven for visiting rabbis, *chassidim* and travelers. One morning his Rebbetzin noticed a new guest in her home and realized that he must have arrived late the previous night. "I didn't make up a bed for you," she said apologetically. "Where did you sleep?"

The visitor explained that the Rebbe had grandly welcomed him into the house and then had hastily excused himself. After a little while, the guest had grown concerned for the Rebbe and eventually discovered him in a bedroom on the third floor of the house, preparing a bed.

To the amazement of all, the Rebbe had climbed the two flights of stairs and, relying exclusively on his sense of touch, had gathered the linens and prepared the bedding. There was no limit to the lengths to which he would exert himself in order to spare a guest the unpleasant feeling of having imposed.

An ardent lover of *Eretz Yisrael*, the Rebbe retained the customs and dress of his native Jerusalem throughout his lifetime. It was very clear to him and to all who met him that residence outside of the Land of Israel, however long its duration, must be viewed and perceived as temporary. In accord with his wishes, his remains were interred in the Mount of Olives in 1946.

It was left to his elder son, Reb Moshe Halevi (1910-1986), to carry on his illustrious father's traditions in New York, and to the Rebbe's younger son, Reb Levi Yitzchak (b. 1921), to return Bostoner *chassidus* to where it had begun — Boston, Massachusetts.

The success of Bostoner *chassidus* is due largely to its unique ideology. Like all Polish *chassidus*, it stresses a close connection between the Rebbe and *chassid*, and views the relationship as a two-way mirror: The *chassid* looks at his Rebbe and sees in him a glimpse of his own potential for greatness, while the Rebbe returns his gaze and derives satisfaction and fulfillment from the spiritual growth of his *chassidim*.

The famed Reb Menachem Mendel of Kotzk, one of the early developers of Polish *chassidus*, literally drove away overly dependent *chassidim*. Although it is in consonance with the Kotzker doctrine, Bostoner *chassidus* maintains that since the most essential attribute is the ability to translate theory into practice, any way in which the Rebbe himself can further this goal is deemed worthwhile. The original Bostoner Rebbe and his sons have always preferred to achieve this ideal through example rather than instruction, and every chapter of their lives has imparted powerful and inspiring lessons.

*

Born in Boston and educated in New York and Jerusa-

lem, Reb Levi Yitzchak,* the Bostoner Rebbe of today, has
radically transformed the role of the chassidic rebbe to
adapt to American realities. He was the first chassidic
rebbe whose primary language of communication is English. In the tradition of Reb Moshe Leib of Sassov he has
focused his activities on reaching out, most particularly to
the college communities which populate Boston. The
Rebbe's efforts have borne rich fruit, as evidenced by the
flourishing, vibrant community whose heart is the New
England Chassidic Center on Beacon Street in Brookline,
Massachusetts.

Within the hallowed halls of the Chassidic Center,
where *minyanim* and *shiurim* are held daily, a host of other
activities also takes place. The projects range from gala
*Shabbaton*s for college students to the tedious work of
R.O.F.E.H., the Rebbe's medical agency which handles
medical liaison, diagnostic referrals, and hospitality for
those who accompany their ailing relatives to any of Boston's outstanding medical facilities. Each venture is personally overseen by the Rebbe himself.

The New England Chassidic Center (Beth Pinchos) is
actually the third of its kind. The first, on Poplar Street in
Boston's West End, was purchased in 1916 by Reb Pinchos
Dovid. His younger son, Reb Levi Yitzchak, was born
there. The second Chassidic Center, on Columbia Road in
the Dorchester section of Boston, was purchased shortly
before the passing of Reb Pinchos Dovid, and went into

---

* The Rebbe's full name, Reb Levi Yitzchak ben Sara Sasha, is identical
to that of his illustrious forebear, Reb Levi Yitzchak (ben Sara Sasha) of
Berditchev.

operation in 1944. The Brookline Chassidic Center was established in 1961.

Since the Chassidic Center features prominently in this book, a brief physical description will aid the reader. Built in 1890, it is situated on Beacon Street, the main thorough-fare of Brookline — a sprawling residential area of Boston where many Orthodox Jews live. In the basement of this five-story structure is a *mikveh*, an oven for matzah-baking, a kitchen and a large social hall. The ground floor houses the *shul* and *ezras nashim*, a study corner and a library; on the next floor is the Rebbe's study, the Chassidic Center office, the R.O.F.E.H. office, the Rebbe's library, the Reb-betzin's kitchen and the dining room; the fourth floor is divided between the Rebbe's residence and guest rooms; and the fifth floor is reserved exclusively for guests. R.O.F.E.H. recently acquired a separate eight-apartment building at 1730 Beacon Street.

Part and parcel of the Chassidic Center for many years was the resident custodian and watchman, Leibel Singer, *z"l*, an old family retainer and general factotum whom the Rebbe's father had literally picked off the street and brought into his home. To provide Leibel with the feeling that he was earning his keep, he was assigned odd jobs and, when necessary, given busy work. The "Leibel" fea-tured in several of this book's stories is actually a composite character of Singer and the occasional assistants the Rebbe has had throughout the years. For this reason the fictitious last name "Wattstein" was substituted.

*

In 1984, precisely fifty years after the Rebbe's father attempted *aliyah*, Boston *chassidus* established a foothold

in the Land of Israel, the fulfillment of Reb Pinchos Dovid's dream and the culmination of many years of frustrated efforts and false starts.

The first of these efforts was made in 1934 when the
Rebbe's father purchased 90 dunams (22.5 acres) of land
near Nebi Samwil (the burial place of the prophet Samuel,
known by its Arabic name) on the outskirts of Jerusalem,
with the intention of building a Bostoner community on
that site.

The Arab uprising of 1936, followed by World War II
and Israel's War of Independence, prevented the project
from getting under way. The Nebi Samwil region was
captured by Jordan in 1948 and only returned to Israeli
jurisdiction in June of 1967, after the Six-Day War.

Return of the land to Israel, however, did not mean
return of the property to Boston, for this, like all other
liberated land, was subsumed under the Right of Eminent
Domain, and the Government became its sole realtor. A
minuscule fraction of the land's value was paid to the
Rebbe by the Israeli Government as token compensation,
and for a short while there was nominal cooperation from
the authorities in assisting Boston to find a different site
for its community.

The Rebbe's fervent desire to actualize his father's plan
to found Boston-Jerusalem resulted in an annual trip to
the Holy Land devoted to investigating possibilities. One
notable near miss, offered by the late Israel Minister of
Finance Pinchas Sapir, was the area contiguous with the
Arab-populated Nebi Samwil, a site now known as Ramot
Polin. This ambitious development plan, like numerous
others, fell through at the last minute.

In 1979 the Rebbe entered into negotiations on a neighborhood which would later be called Har Nof. The original idea was to erect several large buildings to serve as the nucleus of a Bostoner community, and to convert one of the apartments into a *shul*.

This plan, like practically everything else affiliated with the early stages of Har Nof, ran into difficulties because the Government failed to exercise control over the private contractors who were given free reign to develop the area. Without official regulations and jurisdiction, construction advanced only when the contractors deemed it profitable.

Accordingly, laborers and equipment were diverted to other projects and Har Nof was pitifully crippled. Buildings whose completion deadline had long since passed were still on the drawing board, some were abandoned midway, and others had only a barren foundation pit as a testimony to the buyers' naivete. Millions of dollars were invested in what appeared to be bogus deals, and whoever could withdrew and sought a more stable neighborhood to call home.

Enter the Bostoner Rebbe. The first thing the Rebbe did was insist that the Government compel the contractors to adhere to their commitments. Second, the Rebbe and a core of *chassidim* established residence in the nascent neighborhood. Third, the Givat Pinchas *shul* (the largest synagogue in Har Nof) was erected with the help of the late Yosef Gadish, the Deputy Mayor of Jerusalem (see photo section for the full story).

These three things happening concurrently brought about a complete turnaround in the development of Har Nof, today one of the largest religious neighborhoods in

Jerusalem. From the time the Rebbe moved into Har Nof, growth burgeoned at such a rapid pace that he no longer saw a need for separate buildings inhabited exclusively by Bostoner *chassidim*, and adherents purchased and rented apartments wherever they pleased.

With the construction of Givat Pinchas came a *mikveh* and a *kollel*, vital signs of a thriving community, and everyone began to take notice, *including* the contractors. They realized that Har Nof was a lucrative development after all, and they began to complete their initial projects and erect additional buildings at a feverish pace to try and keep up with the demand for housing.

Since the establishment of the Bostoner community in Har Nof, the Rebbe has divided his time between America and Israel. Logic and climatic considerations should theoretically place the Rebbe in Jerusalem during the winter and in Boston during the summer; in practice, however, the opposite obtains. With his *kiruv* activities in Boston linked to the academic calendar, the Rebbe feels compelled to remain in America from October through March. During the spring and summer months, when things slow down in America, he returns to Har Nof.

The Rebbe has three sons — Reb Pinchos Dovid, Reb Mayer and Reb Naftali, and two daughters — Rebbetzin Shayna Frankel and Rebbetzin Toby Geldzahler. Reb Mayer, formerly *Rav* of the Chassidic Center, is currently *Rav* of Givat Pinchas. Rabbi Moshe Chaim Geldzahler is *dayan* of the Boston-Jerusalem community. Reb Pinchos Dovid is the Chuster *Rav* in Boro Park, Brooklyn, a position which he inherited from his father-in-law, Rabbi Yehoshua Greenwald, *zt"l*. Rebbetzin Frankel is the wife of the Vielopeler Rebbe, Reb Yosef Frankel, who is also a prominent *Rav* in the Flatbush section of Brooklyn. Reb Naftali has succeeded Reb Mayer as *Rav* of the Chassidic Center in Brookline.

Since 1983 the Rebbe has served on the presidium of Agudath Israel of America, and in November 1988 he was appointed a member of the *Moetzes Gedolei Hatorah* of *Eretz Yisrael*.

The Milk of
Human Kindness

How do you do that?" Leibel gawked.

"There's nothing to it," Prilluck replied, re-adjusting his fingers on the cow's udder and aiming another squirt of milk into the pail. "All you need to do is put your shoulder to the wheel."

"What?!" Wattstein spluttered, his jaw gaping.

"It's just an expression," the farmer soothed. As the milk pail rapidly filled with foamy white liquid, Prilluck kept up a running commentary. "My beloved father, rest his soul, used to say, 'Unless we strive to live in the Land flowing with milk and honey,'" he quoted, "'we can't expect to enjoy these Divine gifts without striving.'" Leibel nodded his head as though he understood and continued to watch in "udder" fascination as the farmer dexterously relieved the bovine of her burden.

When the pail was full, Prilluck added its contents to Leibel's can, clamped the lid in place, and handed over the five-gallon canister with such ease, it might have been empty. Leibel nearly keeled over when he hefted it.

They met often. An unlikely couple to be sure, but really not all that more disparate than any other two of the Rebbe's* *chassidim*. Leibel Wattstein, a pallid, pint-sized, bespectacled former vagrant, was unemployed for a living, but on the side he served as the self-appointed security man and general factotum of the Chassidic Center, a post he filled with unrivaled dedication, not to mention enthusiasm. Leibel was the proverbial cop who is never around when you need him, and Jack-of-all-trades but master of none.

Yontel Prilluck, a rugged, barrel-chested, bandy-legged old-timer of indeterminate age, was a dairy farmer for a living, but on the side he was the self-appointed *Cholov Yisroel*-dispenser for all of New England. Unlike the conventional farmer in dungaree overalls and flannel shirt, Prilluck wore the garb of a devout urban Jew. He did, however, milk cows, candle eggs and grow tomatoes — but his primary activity was performing boundless acts of lovingkindness.

Although Leibel's attire — a navy poplin uniform with a gold crest embroidered on the shirt pocket and sleeve — was designed to mimic that of an officer of the law, any resemblance to Boston's Finest ended there. On his meanest days this ferret-eyed, lily-livered, jelly-spined pussycat was scared of his own shadow, which made him a natural to guard the premises of the New England Chassidic Center.

Leibel, like Yontel, was by nature a very generous indi-

* The first Bostoner Rebbe, Rabbi Pinchos Dovid Horowitz, *zt"l*.

vidual, and the greatest beneficiary of their *chessed* was the Bostoner Rebbe. In accord with his self-effacing nature, Farmer Prilluck would be the first to deny this and counter that he received far more from the Rebbe than he could ever pay back. But Leibel was a different story altogether.

Years ago the Rebbe had collected Wattstein off the street and provided him with room, board and companionship. So that Leibel shouldn't feel like a freeloader, the Rebbe asked him to keep an eye on the premises, a tragicomic assignment considering the fellow's unintrepid disposition. The Rebbe had never meant it seriously, and certainly never meant for Leibel to go out and find himself a uniform, but wearing it made Leibel feel important — so much so that he was convinced the Chassidic Center would fall to ruin without him and the residents would be robbed blind. Only for so serious a mission as collecting the *Cholov Yisroel* would he dream of abandoning his post.

As the Rebbe's *Cholov Yisroel*-fetcher, Wattstein had witnessed the milking procedure numerous times, but he never ceased to be amazed by it. "How do you get the cow to cooperate?" he inquired in awe. "I would hate to be squeezed like that."

Yontel chuckled. "My sainted mother, may she rest in peace, often repeated the Talmudic saying: 'More than the calf wishes to suckle, the cow wishes to provide.' And believe me, Bracha here is one good provider. She's my *mitzvah* cow," he said, giving the beast an affectionate pat on the rump. "She performs more *mitzvos* in a week than a lot of Jews in the area do in a lifetime." Prilluck handed over the precious milk can, along with a dozen Grade A Jumbos. "Here, Leibel, take these eggs for the Rebbetzin.

She'll find none fresher anywhere. And this cheese — I make it myself."

"But...but...," Wattstein protested, knowing his wallet was empty.

"Never mind," the farmer said with a grin. "My dear father, of blessed memory, always taught me to give with an open hand.

"Please send my best to the Rebbe," Yontel called as Leibel waved goodbye and staggered down the dirt path to the highway.

This was the most difficult part for Leibel: hitching a ride back from farmland to Boston. Stopping a passing car and accepting a lift from a total stranger required more courage than he could ever hope to possess. The aura of officialdom with which his uniform endowed him quickly evaporated at the sight of a redneck truck driver, or any driver, for that matter, other than a little old lady from Passaic — and what little old lady would stop for a hitchhiker?

Once some long-haired hippies in a psychedelic-painted van offered Leibel a ride and by the time he reached the Chassidic Center, he was suffering from a temporary hearing loss caused by the decibel level of the blaring radio, his head swam from the fumes of whatever it was they'd been smoking, and his trembling hands had churned the milk into butter. On another occasion he was picked up by a real policeman and he'd had a hard time, both in the squad car and later at headquarters, explaining what he was doing impersonating an officer of the law.

More recently, Leibel found himself literally in the middle of a police dragnet. An armed robber had frustrated a police- and F.B.I.-chase when he fled from his getaway car and began to make his way on foot through the Massachusetts farmland. The fugitive's high-powered rifle, however, was no match for the arsenal which the State Troopers had at their disposal and poor Leibel was caught in the crossfire.

With his ammunition nearly spent, the crook emerged from a pine grove to find the uniformed Wattstein at the roadside, cowering behind his milk canister in the dim predawn light. The jig is up, he thought, and threw down his weapon and raised his hands. "Don't shoot!" he cried, surrendering himself to Leibel, of all people.

In moments the two were surrounded by shotgun-toting Troopers, and Leibel fainted dead away.

ONE MONDAY, as Leibel was preparing for his biweekly pilgrimage out to the farm, the Rebbe received word that there was no point in his going: Yontel had returned his holy soul to his Maker. The Rebbe was profoundly saddened by the news, but Leibel's grief knew no bounds. Their sole consolation was the size of the *levayah*. Funerals in Boston were generally small, but throngs had gathered to pay their last respects to Reb Yontel Prilluck.

Fighting back his tears, the venerable Rebbe ascended to the podium to bid a final farewell to his beloved farmer, the man who had so graciously and faithfully provided *Cholov Yisroel* products for the Boston community.

"*Rabbosai*," the Rebbe commenced, "I have come to recount the incredible lovingkindness of Reb Yontel Prilluck, a man of rare virtue. Reb Yontel lived to be almost one hundred years old. No doubt he merited the blessing of old age because of his meticulousness in performing the *mitzvos* and his endless acts of *chessed*. We were all witness to and beneficiaries of Reb Yontel's magnanimity, but why have we not sought to emulate him? Why are so few imbued with a giving nature such as his?

"Thousands of Jewish immigrants landed on these hospitable shores, yet those who continued to adhere to the life style we had cherished so dearly in Europe were few in number. Why is it that the influences of America which defiled and corrupted so many of our People did not tarnish Yontel Prilluck?

"Consider his philanthropy, and then contemplate the sorry state of our own. Many of us grudgingly part with one tenth of our income for charity, while Reb Yontel gladly disbursed far, far more.

"For decades Reb Yontel tended to our needs; no chore was ever too difficult for him, no task a burden. He never complained or uttered even the slightest *krechtz*. Where did this humble, unlettered Jew learn to be a *tzaddik*? Surely he inherited his outstanding *middos* from his parents, but of their deeds we shall never know. We can but learn how vital it is that we set the finest example possible for our children, for that is our only hope of producing a generation with the qualities of Yontel Prilluck."

The Rebbe left the podium and a distinguished gentleman rose to speak. He was the Rabbi of a neighboring community. "My dear brothers and sisters," the Rabbi began in a barely audible tone, "I can confirm everything the Rebbe has said. I heard this story from someone who was Reb Yontel's *lantsman* and knew his sainted parents well." A hushed gasp rippled through the crowd.

"In their village in White Russia, Reb Yontel's father earned his living from the manufacture of washboards. It was half a century before the introduction of automatic washing machines in the West, and decades more before they appeared in Russia. Every household in the area was equipped with at least one washboard. Half of the year, old man Prilluck would gather the wood for the boards, and the other half he devoted to converting the raw material into a versatile scrubbing surface. The production of these boards was a family project and every Prilluck family member did his share. The inventory was stored in a small shed in the Prilluck's backyard.

"Late one night Yontel's parents were awakened by a frightful noise behind their house. They leaped out of bed, and peered out the window to discover a thief making off with all of their boards!

"Yontel's father was about to scream for help and alert the neighbors, but his wife quickly silenced him. 'Don't you see who it is?' she whispered urgently. 'Think before you shout. He has two daughters to marry off, and if word of his stealing gets out, no one will ever be interested in them.'

"With Hillelian strength Prilluck contained himself and held his peace; he realized that his wife spoke the truth. This was faint consolation, however, for his business was now in ruins.

"With all of his merchandise gone, he had no way of supporting his family. Barring a miracle, the Prillucks would go hungry that winter.

"With no recourse, Yontel's father scratched together his last few kopeks and purchased tickets for his family to travel to America. Maybe, they prayed, on the other side of the ocean they would be able to realize the hopes and dreams that had been dashed by the robbery.

"The Prillucks did not emigrate to America in order to mine the gold with which the streets were paved. They came so that they might live with dignity; they came so that a thief could marry off his daughters with honor.

"Family and friends," the Rabbi said, lifting a handkerchief to dab at his tear-filled eyes, "this was the legacy that Reb Yontel, *z"l*, inherited from his parents. He never forgot their awesome *mesirus nefesh* nor did he forget how the Almighty rewarded his upstanding parents for their act of courage: Had they not been forced to flee to America, they would surely have fallen victims to the Nazis when the Germans overran White Russia.

"Reb Yontel always felt that since God had been so kind to his family, he was especially obliged to be kind to His People. May his memory be a blessing and an inspiration for us all."

Charring Squad

Passover preparations in a rebbe's home make the conventional household cleanup operation seem like a vacation at Grossinger's. Everything, whether it has come in contact with *chametz* or not, is scrubbed and polished until it shines. Anything which can be dismantled is taken apart and scoured. But the decontamination campaign, laborious as it is, is trivial compared to the ordeal of food preparation. In the 1930s, the unavailability of kosher-for-Passover food products, compounded with the halachic stringencies which are part and parcel of a Chassidic court, mandated that everything to be eaten at the Rebbe's* table had to be prepared in-house.

Even the salt was the Rebbe's own special concoction, guaranteed *chametz*- and fancy-free. This erstwhile seasoning underwent a dramatic metamorphosis in the matzah oven of the Chassidic Center, where any vestige of *chametz*

---

* The first Bostoner Rebbe, Rabbi Pinchos Dovid Horowitz, *zt"l.*

was mercilessly burnt off. What remained was a solid block of *black* halite which resembled agglomerated pepper but had the flavor of barbecued salt.

The manufacture of pepper was an engineering feat no less involuted than its table companion's. Since dried black peppercorns were unobtainable, their botanical cousin, cayenne, was co-opted as a somewhat spicy substitute. The cayenne, a fiercely hot red pepper, had to be ground up manually. Hand-grinding these virulent vegetables was a job for volunteers only, but few volunteers could be found. During the entire process, the grinder's eyes had to be covered to protect them from the acrid fumes; the odor and distinctive coloration were impervious to any cleansing agent known to man and the valorous volunteer would carry them with him for many days as a badge of courage.

Leibel Wattstein, usually eager to comply with any request the Rebbe made, would not go near this one, so the task fell to the immediate family by default.

A time-honored Chassidic stringency is not to use tap water during Pesach. This custom originated in the medieval period, when hostile Gentiles would systematically contaminate the water supply with *chametz* by dropping loaves of bread or bread crumbs into the wells. Since the pollution of water is still possible in contemporary times by intentional or accidental means, *chassidim* customarily drink only water which has been collected before the holiday. Adhering to this stringency entailed the construction, filling, *shlepping* and storing of large tin vats from which the water was drawn throughout the Festival.

There were also vats which held the *mayim shelanu* used for preparing the matzah dough. Attended by many Bostoner *chassidim* and avid onlookers, the drawing of the *mayim shelanu* by the Rebbe from the Boston Reservoir was always an occasion accompanied by great fanfare and spectacle.

The most noteworthy activity of the Passover preparations was the baking of the *shemurah matzos*, a process initiated on *Rosh Chodesh Nissan*. This procedure, from the primary cleansing of the baking tools to the final separation of *challah*, was performed under the strict supervision of the Bostoner Rebbe.

An old-fashioned, wood-burning brick oven had been constructed in the Chassidic Center's basement, and several *chassidim* became rather adept at stoking and tending the fire. Baking was an arduous task but all of the residents of the Chassidic Center (excluding Leibel, who was terrified of fire) participated in this special *mitzvah*.

With the matters of house-cleaning, water-drawing, spice-grinding and matzah-baking well in hand, the Rebbe would turn his attention to the provision of meat. The local ritual slaughterer at the time was a man upon whom the Rebbe was reluctant to rely, but to hire a different *shochet* would be a terrible affront. All year 'round, the Rebbe preferred to abstain from eating meat, but for Pesach and Sukkos, red meat was considered a special *Yom Tov* treat; providing it without insulting the local *shochet* meant engaging in a clandestine operation.

A week or so before the Holiday, sometime after midnight when the eyes of curious neighbors and conscientious health department inspectors were sure to be tightly closed, a calf was smuggled into the basement of the Chassidic Center. Needless to say, spiriting 500 recalcitrant pounds of meat-on-the-hoof down a flight of stairs in a residential building in the dead of the night was no facile endeavor. Once the "little dogie" had been coaxed through the doorway and had clattered down the cellar steps, sentries were posted to keep it company and keep its mooing to a minimum. A considerable helping of prayer enhanced this effort.

Until the deed was actually done, the mood around the house was tense. The old Chassidic Center was located in Boston's West End and even in the 1930s this was a run-down, turbulent neighborhood. Local toughs made frequent forays onto the premises, doing their part to make life miserable, and the cost of repairing the damage they caused was a heavy burden. The Rebbe knew that the family had to vacate soon, but finances made relocation impossible. These were the Depression years and real estate values were as depressed as everything else. The sale of the building could never yield enough for even a down payment in a better part of town, so for the time being, they were stuck with their delapidated facility. The last thing they needed was trouble from the authorities.

NO ONE was more aware of the Rebbe's housing dilemma than Shea Freidlander, a devoted, though somewhat cynical, *chassid*. Through his generosity, the Chassidic Center was covered by a $10,000 fire-insurance policy, a veritable fortune in those days, and not a day would go by without Shea praying for a fire to break out. He fervently wished that the ruffians would abandon their annoying, costly pastime of hurling rocks through the windows, and graduate to arson. At every communal function, Freidlander would urge the Rebbe to offer a benediction for a *gezunte bren* — not one in which anyone might be injured, God forbid, but one destructive enough to warrant collecting the fire insurance. Shea Freidlander was a one-man "charring squad," you might say, and so devoted to this cause that he insisted the Rebbe determine that there was no copy in the house of *Raziel Hamalach*, a Kabbalistic work reputed to ward off fires. The Rebbe always laughed off his *chassid*'s pyrophilial remarks, but in his heart he knew that only a *gezunte bren* could extricate his family from their tenement surroundings.

A few days before Passover, Freidlander visited the Chassidic Center to place his *shemurah matzah* order. When he saw the Rebbe and several *chassidim* tinkering with the flue of the matzah oven, his eyes dilated with anticipation and a cunning smile twitched at the corners of his lips. "I like my *matzos* burnt black," Shea said, and suggested they leave the flue closed for a few hours. "Why don't you join me outside for some fresh air," he joked, "while the oven solves all your problems?"

The Rebbe gave Shea a look of admonition. He didn't find any joke associated with the *mitzvah* of baking *matzos* amusing.

The Sages teach that prophecy today is in the hands of fools and children. And although Freidlander qualified as neither, he was definitely onto something when he placed his matzah order.

ONE WEEK LATER was a momentous day in the lives of Bostoner *chassidim*. Not only was it the day that the calf was to be slaughtered, but it was also the day of the great small fire.

Sometime during the morning hours, a flame leaped out of the oven and ignited a nearby pile of logs. The fire spread quickly, engulfing a third of the basement, and fiery tongues licked at the stair treads. "My *matzos!* My *matzos!*" the Rebbe exclaimed. The Rebbetzin, sighting the plumes of smoke rising outside her window, began shrieking, "*Mein kelbaleh! Mein kelbaleh!*" (My calf!). And Leibel rushed up the stairs screaming, "My life! My life!"

A bucket brigade was quickly formed and water drawn from the fortuitously pre-filled vats. But even eight days' worth of water was not enough to slake the fire's thirst. *Kinderlach* with tears in their eyes shuttled up and down the stairs with sloshing pails, kettles, pots and even *netilas yadayim* cups, and poured them into the inferno. Still the fire raged.

Just then Freidlander came to pick up his *matzos*. The sight of black smoke clouds hovering over the Chassidic Center brought a broad smile to his face and a gleam to his eye. Elated, he ran toward the building, but when he realized that the *chassidim* were trying to extinguish the blaze, he went berserk.

"WHAT DO YOU THINK YOU'RE DOING!!??!!" he railed.

"The Rebbe told us," the children whimpered, and then scampered right past him.

Duly inflamed, Freidlander ran downstairs and confronted the Rebbe with pious zeal. "*Dina d'malchusa dina!* The law of the land must be upheld!" he shouted. "Rebbe, you must instruct these sinners to cease their felonious activity at once! Only card-carrying members of the Fire Fighters Union may extinguish fires. The Fire Department will be smoking for a long time over this infringement of their rights.

"Leave everything to me," he went on. "I'll call the Fire Department to deal with this as soon as I get home. I'm sure I have their number somewhere. In the meantime get all of these non-union people out of the way or they might get hurt."

The Rebbe ignored Shea's impassioned plea. "What about my *matzos*?" he countered.

"What about my *kelbaleh*?" the Rebbetzin echoed, trying to shield the calf from the billowing smoke.

Leibel was long gone.

Despondent over the fire's lack of progress, Shea Freidlander tried to block the youthful couriers of the ad hoc fire brigade, but to no avail. The concerted efforts of the *chassidim* succeeded in containing the blaze and saving the fort. Miraculously the Chassidic Center incurred little damage.

In desperation, Freidlander inspected every inch of the basement, hoping to find it worthy of a sizeable insurance claim, but the situation looked bleak. It seemed the only thing that the Chassidic Center would be collecting was a hefty bill from the painter.

Freidlander slapped his hands together in frustration and surveyed the scene a final time. He found the Rebbetzin holding a baby bottle to the calf's mouth with one hand, and caressing the frightened beast with the other. It looked up at her gratefully, its long-eyelashed *kelbene-oigen* moist with tears. The Rebbe, his face reflecting over-whelming relief, was clutching some of the salvaged *matzos* in his hands. This scene of complacent contentment seemed to disturb Shea to no end, and resignedly he slumped into a sooty chair in the yard.

Suddenly, Freidlander began to laugh.

"What, may I ask, do you find so amusing?" the Rebbe challenged his friend.

With some difficulty, Shea managed to regain his com-posure. "Let me tell you a story, Rebbe.

"One year," he began, "just as the Baal Shem Tov sat down to conduct his *Seder*, he began to chuckle. None of the *chassidim* present at his table had the courage to ask what was so amusing, but after the Holiday was over, one close disciple did muster the nerve to question his master. 'Why did the Rebbe laugh at the beginning of the *Seder*?' he asked.

"The Baal Shem Tov explained that he had been privy to something that had transpired simultaneously in the woods of Galicia and in the portals of Heaven. In the forest north of Krasnopoli, the Rebbe told his devoted student, lived a very simple farmer and his equally simple wife. The couple perfectly complemented one another, which was rather fortunate since they lived alone, far removed from any urban dwelling.

"The little of *Halachah* that the farmer, Shraga Shmeryl, knew, he observed meticulously. This sometimes led to comical situations and his being taken advantage of by others. A case in point was Shraga Shmeryl's zealousness to have a poor guest present for the *Seder*. As a child, he had been told that it was an important *mitzvah* to have a poor man at the *Seder* and so he made every effort to comply.

"His early attempts entailed an annual, grueling pre-Passover journey to Krasnopoli. Wandering through the various *battei midrash*, he sought out a beggar who would join him for the *Seder*. After a few years of this, however, word spread and Shraga Shmeryl never had to search for a guest again. The indigent of the area learned that it was well worth the exhausting trip out to the farm, for there they were treated like kings and the *Seder* hospitality was not restricted to only two nights.

"With time, the local *schnorrers* devised a free-loading scam. They claimed that since it was such an arduous journey to the farm, they had to set out well in advance to make sure that they would arrive in time for Passover. Thus, not long after Purim, the first few guests would arrive, soon joined by additional comrades-in-alms.

"Invariably, the freeloaders explained to naive Shraga Shmeryl that a *Seder* invitation included the entire Passover festival, and needless to say a host should not evict his guests the moment a holiday is over. Thus Mr. and Mrs. Shraga Shmeryl had steady company for five straight weeks every spring.

"One year, however, guests failed to arrive after Purim and the simple couple began to worry. *Rosh Chodesh Nissan* rolled around and still no beggars appeared at their door. The farmer was distraught. How would he fulfill the important *mitzvah* of hosting the poor?

"*Shabbos Hagadol* came and went and so did the night of *bedikas chametz*. It was just one day to the *Seder* and the Shmeryls were still all by themselves.

"As Passover eve approached, a pall of sadness overcame the couple. Shraga Shmeryl scaled the tallest tree in the area as the sun was about to set, hoping he might yet spot a vagabond lost on the way, but all of the paths were empty, bare of a living soul. Morose and crestfallen, he sat down at his *Seder* table, but the sight of the tears streaming down his wife's cheeks rendered him unable to commence the service.

"Now this pitiful scene, the Baal Shem Tov explained, caused quite a commotion in Heaven. It was decided in the Celestial Court that a guest would have to be dispatched at once, and who would be more appropriate for this mission than Eliyahu *Hanavi*?

"Just as Eliyahu was preparing for the journey, however, the farmer had an idea. 'Don't worry,' Shraga Shmeryl comforted his wife, 'we will yet have a guest.' The woman straightened herself up expectantly as her husband dashed out of the house and into his barn.

"*Shlepping* a decorative afghan, he approached his favorite pony and gave him a gentle pat on the head. With a jubilant expression on his face and the rapture of victory adding bounce to his step, Shraga Shmeryl led the afghan-draped pony to his table. The farmer threw a solicitous arm around the horse's neck and happily informed his wife that a guest had arrived after all.

"The Angels in Heaven were incredulous at this scene. Immediately they aborted Eliyahu's mission with a cherubic chortle.

"'When I saw the Angels chuckle,' the Baal Shem Tov concluded, 'I could not refrain from laughing myself.'

"My dear Rebbe," Freidlander sighed, "your salvation had already been dispatched from Heaven, yet you sent it an about-face order, just to rescue a doomed calf and a few kilos of poor man's bread! Like the Baal Shem Tov, all I can do is laugh."

Souls at Sea

While America and her allies were jubilantly celebrating V-E Day, American Jewry languished beneath a heavy pall of sorrow and guilt. There was widespread mourning over the annihilation of six million of their brethren, but perhaps even worse, there were daily revelations that gnawed at their conscience. It soon became patently obvious that much, much more could have been done to save thousands and thousands of souls from unspeakable deaths. Jews everywhere pondered the imponderable: Why were *we* privileged to survive?

The Rebbe bore yet another burden, one which lay heavily on his heart. His father had passed away in 1941 and had left explicit instructions that he be buried in the Holy Land, where he had lived in his youth. The Rebbe knew that until his father was reinterred in the plot alongside *his* father, the Rebbe would have no *menuchah*.

A sea voyage, the only available means to this end, was unavoidable. Now that the war was over and transatlantic shipping renewed, the Rebbe became obsessed with carrying out this mission. But as he quickly learned, the termination of hostilities did not automatically open up the sea lanes which had been restricted for nearly six years. The waters were still heavily mined, and civilian passage was limited to a strict quota.

Senator David I. Walsh from Massachusetts was a long-time friend of the family and a powerful member of the Foreign Affairs Committee, which oversaw the issue of transatlantic travel permits. The Rebbe appealed to him to secure the special documentation he would need to make the trip, but it wasn't until the summer of 1946 that permission was granted.

The boat which was to take the Rebbe and his father's remains to *Eretz Yisrael* was the cargo freighter *The Loma Victory*, a name which the Rebbe felt augured well for the success of his journey.

As the date of departure neared, however, the Rebbe grew steadily more apprehensive. A 16-day trip on a crowded freighter promised to be irksome and depressing. Unable to secure travel permits for any of his *chassidim*, the Rebbe was painfully aware that he would not be able to hear the Torah reading or *daven* with a *minyan* for the entire duration of the trip. He prayed that he would find some pleasant company on board, but in his heart of hearts his greatest concern was that there not be *un*pleasant company on board. In that postwar era, anti-Semitism was as rife in America as it was in Europe, only it found more subtle expression in the form of a "gentlemen's agreement" — the tacit collusion of WASPs and other Gentiles to exclude "dogs and Jews," not to mention

"Negroes," from their bastions of society. By making this foray out of the sheltered chassidic community, the young Rebbe knew he was placing his welfare in the hands of less than sympathetic, and possibly overtly hostile, elements.

When the Rebbe boarded the freighter, he found that passengers and crew together totaled only twelve, thereby reducing the chances of one of his fellow travelers being a Jew, someone with whom he might casually pass the time of day. Attired in his distinctive chassidic garb, the Rebbe had little hope of being unobtrusive, and as the passengers all scrutinized one another, he became the primary object of their interest.

The Rebbe, who had always considered himself a student of human nature, commenced his own analysis. With no obvious signs such as *yarmulke* or *tzitzis* to go by, determining which, if any, of them was Jewish presented quite a challenge. Mentally he began the process of elimination.

The crew, by virtue of their chosen profession but more because of their demeanor, were canceled out immediately, leaving seven other passengers yet to identify. Carlos Ricardo Martinez and Salvatore Tarascanbolo, it was reasonable to assume, were not members of the Tribe. Likewise a grossly robust man with glittering eyes like chips of green agate, a washboard paunch, and the shoulders and forearms of a gladiator. He looked as if he could tear telephone books in sixteenths, or allow automobiles to drive over his expansive chest and escape unharmed. The Rebbe had never seen anyone of those proportions before — in or out of the *beis midrash*.

When a fellow passenger exchanged a blatantly anti-Semitic gibe with this muscle-man, yet another candidate was eliminated from the Rebbe's "Who is a Jew" list. At the same time, that slur heightened his initial anxiety for his own well-being. Jokes such as the one shared by those two have a nasty way of being unfunny, particularly to the butt of this so-called humor and particularly when no effort is made by the comedians to avoid being overheard.

What would happen, the Rebbe dared not contemplate, if He-Man decided that shuffleboard wasn't entertaining enough and he sought other, more amusing diversions? What would happen if a storm were to erupt and it was deemed necessary to jettison "excess baggage"? Only the Rebbe's faith in the Almighty and confidence in the merit of his sainted father allayed his fears that he might suffer Jonah's seagoing trials.

The remaining passengers on the boat appeared to be relatively mild-mannered, and although he had no firm evidence, the Rebbe suspected that all three of them were Jews. They simply did not look like Gentiles.

Walter Landon was only about forty-five, but his hairline was long gone. His serious, unlined face was thin and dignified. He had the look of a humble shopkeeper, with his threadbare summer-weight business suit and old-fashioned tie, and there was an aura about him of preoccupation: although his body was on the boat, his mind seemed a million miles away. Perhaps business was bad.

Then there was Norman Manes, who effected a freshly-trimmed vandyke that drew his portly pink face to a point. The first few creases of age added character to his countenance, but not particularly good character. With that faintly superior look in his eyes and that arrogant, self-important bearing, the Rebbe thought him a typical *maskil*.

Mark Cole, the youngest and quietest of this motley bunch, was so reserved that conversation virtually had to be drawn out of him. He was the ideal counterpoint to some of the others, who were quick to pour out their life story, in lurid detail, at the first opportunity. Although Mark had a wholesome, "All-American boy" look, the Rebbe sensed that he too was Jewish.

Later that evening, over dinner, the Rebbe had a chance to test out his theories. He had deliberated for quite a while over whether or not he should join the other passengers in the mess hall for the meal. Certainly his curiosity about his shipmates' identities could not legitimize his breaking bread in a *treif* dining room, and to this day the Rebbe cannot call to mind any other place which so effectively diminished his appetite. And yet, and yet....

Since eating was a necessity, and the limited supply of canned kosher meat and powdered eggs and milk he had brought along would not suffice for the entire trip, the Rebbe decided to repair to the galley in search of some supplemental fruit, vegetables and liquid refreshment. At the same time, he did not wish to call additional attention to himself by being the only one absent from the meals.

Although the Rebbe hardly expected to find another *kashrus*-observing individual on board, he had a hunch that *what* the passengers ordered and *how* they ordered it would be revealing. Just as his choice of menu would speak volumes to them, theirs would surely provide him with further insights into their background and affiliation.

The Rebbe headed for the extreme end of the mess hall and would have made it to the foot of the small, narrow table had Norman not called out, "*Nu, Rebbe, zetz zich avek.*"

He pulled out the chair to his right and motioned for the Rebbe to join him.

One down and two to go, the Rebbe mused.

Not much later, Mark Cole entered and seated himself opposite the Rebbe, confirming his suspicions about the young man's Jewishness. Were he a Gentile, the Rebbe told himself, the "All-American boy" would have kept his distance, especially since there were a number of vacant seats.

Walter-the-shopkeeper, who had removed his jacket but retained his grease-stained tie, chose the chair opposite Norman-the-*maskil*, but by the time he'd entered this was actually the only empty place. Indeed before he sat down he made a show of scanning the length of the room, to demonstrate that he was sitting with this particular group merely because it was the only vacancy. To drive the point home, he sat down with a helpless shrug.

Despite Walter's nonverbal disclaimers, the Rebbe still believed him to be a coreligionist — if not in practice, then at least by birth. If his conjectures were in fact true, then he was about to partake of his first shipboard meal in the company of three Jews, a somewhat better prospect than eating with *goyim*, and this thought lifted the Rebbe's spirits. The Sages say: A son — even a wayward son — remains a son nonetheless.

Norman broke the ice with a pointed philosophical discourse. He toyed with the nadir of his vandyke and commented wryly, "Religion is a funny thing, don't you think? I have always taken for granted my position as a garden-variety, Freudian-based rationalist and therefore find it shocking to encounter someone who still adheres to

The Rebbe's uncle, R. Yehoshua Horowitz, a noted Jerusalem Kabbalist and a sixth-generation descendant of R. Shmelka of Nikolsberg.

The Rebbe's uncle, R. Nochum Brandwein, a sixth-generation descendant of the Baal Shem Tov.

The Rebbe's grandmother, Rebbetzin Shayna Elka Horowitz, daughter of R. Elazar Mendel of Lelov.

4. The Rebbe, *right*, with his sister, Rebbetzin Faiga Thumim, *left*, and their mother, ca. 1930.

5. The Rebbe's father, with his *gabbai*, R. Leo H. Baumel, and older brother, 1929, upon departure for Israel. This photo was taken on board *The St. Louis,* the same boat which later transported Jewish refugees rejected by U.S. immigration authorities back to Europe.

6. Leibel in "uniform" with the Rebbe at age 4 in his chassidic attire.

7. The Rebbe at age 4.

8. The Rebbetzin as a child.

9. Elizabeth Peabody House, ca. 1915, the first Chassidic Center in Boston's West End, where the Rebbe was born.

10. The Rebbe's mother, Sara Sasha, prepares to light the candles in the *sukkah* of the first Chassidic Center in Boston's West End, 1927. The Rebbe, age 6, is holding his ears in anticipation of the loud POP! the photographer's flash powder would make.

11

54

11. In 1934 the Rebbe's father, Reb Pinchos Dovid, attempted *aliyah*. The family moved into a spacious apartment on the second floor of a three-story building on Shmuel Hanavi Street in Jerusalem. One of the distinctive features of this two-family house was that on the ground floor lived the British Mandatory Governor of Jerusalem, a man who displayed little appreciation for *his* distinguished neighbors. Every day, when the Rebbe's family conducted their daily *minyan*, the Governor would run upstairs to lodge a complaint about the disturbance. And as the complaints increased in frequency and intensity, the Rebbe decided it would be best to relocate.

The apartment was to be taken over by a large Arab family, whose religion dictated the time permissible for their move. As it happened, that date conflicted with the Rebbe's scheduled departure: the Rebbe was to vacate on a Sunday but the Arab family needed to move in on the preceding Friday.

A simple, although somewhat unorthodox, solution to this dilemma was found when the head of the Arab household asked if his family might move into the Rebbe's home on the Friday, and the Rebbe agreed. A temporary barrier was erected, dividing the apartment between East and West.

For forty-eight hours, the two families coexisted in harmony, each family "doing their own thing." *Minyanim* were conducted as usual on the Rebbe's side, while multiple prostrations and invocations to Allah were conducted on the other. This stereophonic disturbance to his Governorship impelled him to send for reinforcements, and soon a visible military presence was bivouacked on Shmuel Hanavi Street. Neither family seemed terribly perturbed, however, and they passed their weekend peacefully.

Over Shabbos, the Rebbetzin ventured across the living room to visit her counterpart, who turned out to be a woman of her own distinctive *yichus* — she was the sister of the Emir Abdullah, later King Abdullah who was assassinated on the steps of the Dome of the Rock. (His grandson King Hussein currently reigns over Jordon.) The Rebbetzin offered a friendly warning about their downstairs neighbor.

"Oh, I know him," the Arab matriarch said, dismissing him with a flick of her wrist. "We all know him, and despise him. I assure you that after one week of us, he will be pining for you and wishing he had you back as his neighbors. After *two* weeks, the matter will be academic: he will never be able to last longer than that."

12. In 1938 the Rebbe was a "camper" at the first Torah camp on the American continent, Camp Mesivta in Ferndale, N.Y., founded by R. Shraga Feivel Mendlowitz. Here the Rebbe strolls with R. Shlomo Heiman, *Rosh Yeshiva* of Torah Vodaath; R. Moshe Leiberman; and R. Mordechai Berkowitz, of Far Rockaway and Har Nof, Jerusalem.

13. Some of Camp Mesivta's earliest "campers," who later became active on the American Torah scene. *Left to right, seated,* R. Nisson Gordon, Yitzchak Karp, Phillip Lerner. *Left to right, standing,* (unidentified), R. Meyer Greenberg of Patterson, N the Rebbe.

14. Soon after his marriage the Rebbe, accompanied by the Lapisher Rav, visited the nascent Lakewood Yeshiva — in a horse-drawn buggy!

13

14

15. The Rebbe, *center*, at the *chassan's tisch* with his brother, R. Moshe, *left*, and the Shotzer Rebbe, *right*, who was *unterferer* for the *kallah*. Note the homemade appearance of the *shtreimlach* of that era.

16. Among the Rebbe's wedding guests were R. Moshe Leiberman, *3rd from right, standing*, who later became *Rosh Yeshiva* of Torah Vodaath; R. Shmuel Teitelbaum, the Chentchkevitzer Rav of Brooklyn, *left, seated*; R. Joel Beer, the Ratzverder Rebbe of Sao Paulo, Brazil, *2nd from right, seated*; and R. Jacob Thumim, now the Altshtetter Rav and brother-in-law of the Rebbe, *right, seated*.

17. When the Rebbe was married in 1942, there were no *glatt* kosher catering facilities adequate to accommodate the large number of guests. Two halls were rented in the Empire Manor in Brownsville, N.Y. (one for the women and one for the men), 1,000 new place settings of china and flatware were purchased for the occasion, and *kashrus* was supervised by the Rebbe's family. Music was provided by the Varshever Kapelia Meister — a non-religious but talented old-world musician who was noted for his distinctive *klezmer* style. The Bostoner *chassidim* taught him their unique *niggunim* for leading the groom to the *badecken*, breaking the glass, after the *chuppah*, *sheva berachos*, etc. Many of these *niggunim* have become so popular over the years that they are played and sung at virtually every religious wedding celebration.

18. The Rebbe's sons,
Mayer, *left*, and
Pinchas.

19. The Rebbe's eldest
son, Pinchas, on the
day his *payos* were
made.

20. Leibel and the Rebbe's son, R. Naftali.

21. The Dorchester Chassidic Center.

22. At all three Chassidic Centers, a special wood-burning matz
oven was constructed for baking *shemurah matzos* for Passov
Mr. Joseph Mael, *center*, the Rebbe's oldest *chassid* (he passe
away at the age of 100) always participated in this *mitzvah*.
Note Leibel (behind Mael), keeping his distance from the f
but anxious as ever to be included in the photo.

23. Yontel Prilluck, who provided *Cholov Yisroel* products for the Rebbe (see "The Milk of Human Kindness").

24. At the First *Mikveh* Dinner in Boston, 1948. *Left to right*, Dr. Benjamin Bahn, a communal and Young Israel leader; R. Benzion Brook, Navarodok *Rosh Yeshiva*; the Talner Rebbe; the Rebbe; Mr. Edward Gerber, a noted attorney; R. J.B. Soloveitchik; Samuel Feuerstein.

25. The Rebbe founded the Boston branch of Agudath Israel.
Here R. Binyamin Zev Handelis, a member of Agudah's
National Presidium, addresses an Agudah gathering in the
Rebbe's *sukkah* in Dorchester, 1957. *Left to right*, R. Handelis;
the Rebbe; R. Mordechai Savitsky, a great Torah scholar; R.
Kalman Lichtenstein of Chelsea; R. Moshe Plotnick of
Dorchester.

the naive precepts of religion after the Nazi experience."

Norman's voice was loud but it was clear that his words were addressed exclusively to his three immediate table-mates. Apparently he too presumed Walter and Mark to be Jews, and he wished to dominate the clique. Like a Forty-second Street sandwich-board advertiser, he continued to broadcast his heresy.

Walter looked at the Rebbe for a reaction; Mark gazed intently ahead. The waiter was hovering and seemed about to interrupt in any case, so the Rebbe chose to consider his response while the others placed their meal orders.

Conspicuously, Norman ordered the smoked ham, spaghetti with meat sauce and "plenty of Parmesan." Walter refused the meat, but accepted a baked potato. With a surreptitious glance at the Rebbe, he specified "no butter or cream, please." All the cooked food was unquestionably non-kosher, but this, the Rebbe surmised, was Walter's way of making accommodation.

Young Mark scanned the limited menu indecisively. "Oh, it doesn't matter," he said at last. "I'll have whatever the others are having."

"Oh, yes," Walter added, "I'd like the soup first." Turning to the Rebbe, he remarked, "It's only vegetable soup, so you don't have to worry."

The Rebbe was somewhat taken aback by this comment. Up until this moment, he had been observing and assessing his shipmates only as an intellectual exercise, playing the sleuth and looking for clues as to their Jewishness. But now that the evidence was arrayed before him and his suspicions were confirmed, he realized that he did indeed "have to worry" — not about his own well-being, but about theirs. Providence had placed him on that boat, at that time, with those men, not only to honor his father but to give a fitting tribute to a man who had devoted his entire life to drawing his fellow Jews closer to their Judaism.

ON THE DECK later that evening, the Rebbe gripped the ship's rail tightly and gazed out upon the vast sea. He recalled the Sages' commentary on *techeles*, the Torah-mandated colored strand of *tzitzis*: that its color is intended to remind the wearer of the blue of the ocean, which in turn brings to mind the blue of the heavens and the Heavenly Throne. Indeed, as he stood beneath the night's star-studded canopy, the sea and the heavens were one.

The Rebbe recited the *Ma'ariv* prayers with great fervor, and when he emerged from his devotions, he knew that this journey had yet another purpose: It was to be a test of his abilities to lead his people. With his father's passing, the mantle of leadership had fallen on his youthful shoulders, but he had yet to prove himself truly worthy. Clearly, Norman, Walter and Mark had significant roles to play.

Upon further reflection, the Rebbe began to see himself and his fellow Jewish passengers as more or less typical of the four types of Jews, traditionally characterized in the Passover *Haggadah* as "The Four Sons." As the journey continued, this simplified classification was borne out by their behavior.

Norman was the "wicked son," who knew the Holy Laws but denied their validity. Despite the Rebbe's attempts to reach out to him, he remained incorrigible. Repeatedly, the Rebbe tried to show him the error of his ways, hoping that Norman was only a "wayward son," but Norman responded with increasing cynicism. He viewed every encounter with the Rebbe as an opportunity to disseminate his antireligious venom. In the end, the Rebbe felt he would have been better off following the preaching of the *maggid*: "Blunt his teeth."

His failure to reach Norman, however, caused the Rebbe enormous distress. Was this an indication that he was unequal to the task that awaited him? Again he turned to the sea for an answer.

The *Midrash* relates the story of a man who falls overboard and plunges into the icy waters. The ship's captain casts him a line and calls: "Just hold on to that rope. As long as you keep holding on, you won't drown, but if you let go, you'll be gone." Norman had disregarded the captain's dire warning. He had let go of the rope that bound him to *Yiddishkeit*, the rope that would have towed him to safety, and now he was gone. Only the Captain of captains could pull him from the depths.

The Rebbe redoubled his efforts with Walter.

Walter, it seemed, was "the simple son," whom the Rebbe had to educate on the most elementary level. His capacity to absorb was limited, as was his receptiveness. Profound philosophical discourses, the Rebbe knew, were not in order here; they would fall on deaf ears. Instead he displayed for Walter the warmth of *chassidus*, and eventually the message touched even his hardened businessman's soul.

Mark was "the son who does not even know how to ask," and after a week-and-a-half of informal learning sessions with him, the Rebbe understood the Sages' admonition that unless one "opens up" this son, he is destined to develop into a "wicked son." Initially Mark had set sail for a nefarious purpose; by the time *The Loma Victory* docked, he had altered his itinerary.

The Rebbe became an anchor for these "souls at sea," not allowing them to drift too far from the safe harbor of their Jewish heritage. After two tempestuous weeks of arguing, discussing, debating and educating, the Rebbe learned what leadership is all about: Leadership is the only ship that cannot seek shelter in a storm. To lead his people, to inspire them to strive for closeness to the Almighty, to imbue them with a love for *Yiddishkeit*, a rebbe had to do more than set a good example. He had to reach out to each and every one, casting aside his fears of rejection and insult, and searching relentlessly for the route to each one's heart.

Journey's end was in fact only the first of many "ports of call" in a voyage that would continue for a lifetime. And when the shores of the Holy Land came into view at last, the Rebbe felt himself a far "wiser son" than when he'd embarked.

Two Hearts that Beat as One

Yedida Rudinsky and Elisheva Lehrer had always been close. Only one year separated the two sisters in age; they were married at about the same time, and their firstborn children had entered the world only minutes apart, although at opposite sides of the globe.

Yedida and Elisheva had much in common. There was little physical resemblance between the two and yet many had trouble telling them apart. Their voices, their gestures, their facial expressions were so alike that even people who knew them both well often confused them. Yes, they had much in common, but the most tragic thing they shared was that their firstborn children both had the same congenital heart defect. Known as tetralogy of Fallot, this disorder renders children cyanotic, that is, they turn blue as a result of respiratory distress and air hunger; they suffer spells of anxiety and altered levels of consciousness when the oxygen level of their blood falls below normal.

The Rebbe's first contact with the sisters was by phone.

Mrs. Rudinsky, a resident of Jerusalem, called from Israel; Mrs. Lehrer, from Chicago. Coincidentally their calls came two days apart and the stories they told were virtually identical. Yedida's four-year-old son, Shmulik, and Elisheva's four-year-old daughter, Shuli, both required urgent corrective cardiac surgery. Knowing of the Rebbe's extensive experience with medical referrals, the sisters had turned to him for guidance.

The Rebbe assured them both that he would make all the arrangements. "My good friend, Professor Aldo Castanada, happens to be the world's foremost pediatric cardiologist," the Rebbe explained, "and he is affiliated with the world's foremost pediatric care facility, Boston Children's Medical Center. I'll do everything I can at this end, and get back to you as soon as possible." Immediately, he contacted the Medical Center and was put through to his friend's office. For the Rebbe, Dr. Castanada — whose services were in great demand — would make himself available.

The Rudinskys and Lehrers arrived as scheduled three weeks before surgery, and since the two fathers had remained behind with their young families, it was only natural that the mothers share a Project R.O.F.E.H. apartment. (R.O.F.E.H. — the acronym for Reaching Out–Furnishing Emergency Healthcare — is a branch of the Chassidic Center which assists people from all over the world who are compelled to seek specialized medical care far from their homes. R.O.F.E.H. provides medical referrals, transportation to and from the hospital, interpreters, moral support, and most importantly, free room and board in a special apartment complex adjacent to the Chassidic

Center for patients and their families.) The children's medical records had been sent on ahead and the operations were to take place on consecutive days, Thursday and Friday, as these were the only two days that Dr. Castanada had open.

DESPITE THEIR five years of separation, the bonds of sisterhood between Yedida and Elisheva were unusually strong. Indeed, the unfortunate burden they'd had to share had drawn the sisters even closer. It was not uncommon to see Yedida feeding her niece Shuli, or Elisheva conducting an animated discussion with Shmulik. Each mothered her sister's child as her own, which increased the Rebbe's confusion as to who was who. Everyone commented on how warmly Yedida and Elisheva cared for one another and for their respective niece and nephew.

Once, when Shmulik tripped on the stairs to the Rebbe's apartment and skinned his knee, Elisheva darted to his aid and tenderly scooped him up in a warm embrace. "Oh, my sweet *yingele*," she crooned, "did you hurt yourself? Here, let me kiss it." The way she cuddled him and the seriousness she awarded to his minor bruise caused the Rebbetzin to remark, "This is a genuine *Yiddishe Mama*. There's no greater love than that of a Jewish mother for her child." It was only later that she realized that Elisheva was Shmulik's aunt.

Actually, Yedida and Elisheva were not the only ones to mother Shmulik and Shuli. These two precious four-year-olds were so incredibly adorable, blessed by their Creator with irresistible charm and a beauty that radiated from their pure souls, that everyone was immediately drawn to them. They both had large, deep-green eyes, the most pinchable cheeks and winsome smiles. Shuli's delicate brown hair was usually fixed in a neat ponytail, and Shmulik had cute little *payos* that curled to his earlobes. They resembled each other far more than their mothers did; they might have been twins.

There is never a shortage of beautiful children at the Chassidic Center, *baruch Hashem*, but from the moment these two little cousins arrived, they captured everyone's heart.

As the long-awaited day drew near, the foursome took up residence at Children's Hospital and they were sorely missed in the Rebbe's home. Most of the week before the operation was devoted to preoperative testing, a time normally fraught with anxiety, but having the emotional and physical support of her sister seemed to alleviate some of the strain of this period for each of the women. That their plight was a shared one was, ironically, a blessing. Throughout all the hardship they had each other, and considering their distance from home and from their husbands' moral support, this was a vital factor.

IN RETROSPECT, one might say that with such a serious operation looming over them, the mothers remained surprisingly cheerful. From the moment they arrived in Boston their moods were upbeat and their spirits high. Aside from the sisters' remarkable *bitachon*, their positive frame of mind was in part a tribute to Dr. Castanada, whose deserved reputation evoked confidence and certainty of success. Undoubtedly the aura of Children's Hospital, which virtually exudes competence and efficiency, also played a major role. But to no small measure the hospitality and comforts provided by R.O.F.E.H. contributed to their ease. This is what R.O.F.E.H. is all about.

The confidence felt and expressed by the mothers was transferred to all, including the Rebbe and the other residents of the Chassidic Center. Lulled into a feeling that all would go well, they greeted the dawn of the Big Day as a harbinger of glad tidings and a rosy future.

On Thursday afternoon the phone rang.

The Rebbe could not believe his ears. He, too, had been inordinately relaxed about the children's fate and the outcome of the surgery. On the phone was a member of Castanada's surgical team notifying the Rebbe that Shmulik, beautiful and pure little Shmulik, had died on the operating table.

Before the Rebbe could recover from the shock, Dr. Castanada's secretary got on the line. "Mrs. Rudinsky asked me to tell you that she is on her way to your residence," she said, "to arrange the transferral of the body to Israel for burial."

The Rebbe was overcome with despair. What could he possibly say to that brave young mother? What words could console her? He knew how much she had looked forward to taking Shmulik back home to *Eretz Yisrael*, to watching him for the first time run and play with all the other *kinderlach* in *Yerushalayim* without the terror that the exertion might worsen his condition. Oh yes, she would be taking him back home, but never would she see him running and playing, never would those deep-green eyes twinkle at her mischievously. The years of anxiety were over...to be replaced by sorrow.

A lump lodged in the Rebbe's throat. He could barely utter a polite thank you to Castanada's secretary. He knew the anguish he felt was infinitesimal alongside Yedida Rudinsky's, and his mind reeled with the awesomeness of his responsibilities. First and foremost were the flight arrangements: In order for the burial to take place as soon as possible and not be delayed by Shabbos, the Rebbe would have to get Yedida and her son's coffin onto the Thursday night flight. There were four scant hours at his disposal.

Four hours. The Rebbe has had to make such arrangements in the past on very short notice, but experience did little to simplify a complex procedure. Getting a death certificate issued was always time-consuming, as was arranging the release of the body from the hospital morgue. New York-bound flights from Boston land at LaGuardia Airport, but flights from New York to Israel leave from Kennedy, necessitating additional coordination of connecting flights. Furthermore not every carrier is willing to carry a coffin.

With a bit of *siyatta d'Shemaya*, everything could be arranged in four hours, but the Rebbe knew very well that the next four hours would not be devoted solely to flight itineraries. He could not postpone the task of comforting Yedida, and at the same time he would have to encourage Elisheva to proceed with Shuli's surgery despite the tragic outcome of her nephew's operation.

Amid the frenetic rush of phone calls, the Rebbe suddenly paused. "If, *chas v'shalom*, I found myself in these circumstances," he wondered aloud, "would there be any words which could convince me to go ahead with the surgery? Perhaps I'm overstepping my bounds by assuming that it is my task to convince her to proceed. Maybe the *opposite* is true. Maybe my obligation is in fact to view Shmulik's demise as a portent, and to *dissuade* Elisheva."

The responsibility weighed heavily upon the Rebbe. He considered the close to four decades of R.O.F.E.H.'s existence. R.O.F.E.H. was created for a specific purpose: to direct patients to the best medical facilities available and to serve as a support system for those in need. "It is not ours to decide what course of action the patients should follow," the Rebbe admonished himself. He prayed that *Hashem* would place the right words in his mouth.

Calling in favors all over town, the Rebbe set the wheels in motion for the orderly transfer of the coffin. The travel agent promised to get back to him and as he nervously awaited the return call, the Rebbetzin appeared at the door to his study, with Elisheva Lehrer at her side. The Rebbe could see that Shuli's mother had been crying, yet he sensed that she had drawn upon an inner reserve of strength. The loss to her had to have been nearly as devastating as to her sister. And then, even before Elisheva was seated, the door to the room opened again, and there was Yedida.

The two sisters fell upon each other and the scene before the Rebbe's eyes defied description. In that intense embrace the sisters seemed to be pouring strength from one to the other. Their tears mingled; words were unnecessary. The Rebbetzin exchanged a look of helplessness with the Rebbe and their eyes too burned with tears.

The sobbing women eventually fell silent and held one another at arm's length, each gazing meaningfully into her sister's eyes. The valor and fortitude of millennia of Jewish womanhood was etched on their faces.

The room was charged with emotion and the moment had come for the Rebbe to fulfill his role, but he felt unequal to the task. He had not learned his lines. He opened his mouth to speak but the weak, sorrowful voice he heard was Yedida's.

"Rebbe," she whispered hoarsely, "I am extremely grateful to you and everyone in your community for everything you've done. Because of you, I had access to the finest medical care available. Had my son been operated on by anyone else, anywhere else, I don't think I would be able to live with myself. Shmulik received the best, but obviously the Healer of all Flesh understands better than we what is right for our children.

"Now I must face the unpleasant task of informing the children in Shmulik's *cheder* that he will not be returning to learn with them, that he has gone to learn Torah from *Hashem* Himself.

"I take comfort in knowing that we did all we could for our child. And tomorrow my sister will do all that *she* can for *hers*.... May *Hakadosh Baruch Hu* guide the surgeon's hand, and yours, dear Rebbe, always."

Material Witness

Reams of papers had accumulated on the Rebbe's desk, all demanding his immediate attention. But before he could decide which matter to tackle first, the telephone rang. It was Leonard Weissbard, a newcomer to Boston who occasionally stopped by the Chassidic Center to catch a *minyan* for *Minchah*. Like any newcomer, Leonard had numerous questions about schooling, shopping, housing, and the conveniences available to the Jewish community, and everyone was trying to help him get acclimated. This time, however, he was in for a disappointment.

Thousands of Bostonians had taken advantage of the President's Day Sale at Filene's Basement and Leonard had been among them. Now he wanted to know where the local *shaatnez* laboratory was, so that he could have his four new suits tested.*

---

* Since the Torah expressly prohibits the wearing of *shaatnez* — garments which contain any interwoven fibers of wool and linen — observant Jews have developed a method of testing fabric for the presence of this forbidden combination.

Naively Leonard had touched a raw nerve. Everyone who moved to New England from New York expected Boston, home to 230,000 Jews and blessed with ample facilities to meet the routine needs of the burgeoning *kehillah*, to have its own *shaatnez* laboratory. In truth most New Yorkers, raised on a religious life of luxury and limitless accommodations, have unrealistic expectations for other communities. They expect to have a choice of restaurants at which to dine, a variety of schools for their youngsters to attend, abundant social activities, and naturally a *shaatnez* laboratory only a short bus ride away.

"I'm sorry," the Rebbe told Leonard, "but we do not have a local facility. You'll have to send the clothes to New York for inspection." As anticipated, Leonard was incredulous.

The Rebbe resumed his perusal of the letters on his desk. He hadn't gotten very far when the phone rang again, this time with a *shailah* from a *chassid*. The subject: *shaatnez*. And no sooner had he hung up the phone, when the Rebbetzin stalked into the study angrily displaying an oversized manila envelope stamped with the insignia of a *shaatnez* laboratory in Brooklyn. "Can you imagine?" she fumed. "I send them a jacket in the original packing from Loehman's, and I get it back in *this!*" She held up the well-traveled, tattered envelope, through the ripped-off corner of which the Rebbetzin's new jacket peeked. "We get junk mail in better condition than this!"

The Rebbe responded with a sigh of resignation.

"All right," the Rebbetzin relented, "I understand. They must have been under tremendous pressure and were eager to return my jacket as quickly as possible. Maybe it was a new worker who didn't know better. One day, with God's help, we'll have our own facility nearby...."

Three queries on the same subject in the space of ten minutes were two coincidences too many. The Rebbe knew that he dared not ignore it. Immediately he set his mind to finding a local solution to the *shaatnez*-testing dilemma.

His first call was to the New York facility, but they were swamped with pre-Holiday orders; their response to his offer of sponsoring a Boston branch of their *shaatnez* lab was understandably less than enthusiastic. With a huge backlog of tests to conduct, they couldn't see past the mountain of clothes which engulfed them to give the Rebbe's request their due consideration. The Rebbe, disappointed but far from discouraged, became more determined than before to pursue the matter to its ultimate resolution.

Suddenly he remembered something a guest had mentioned several years earlier. A graduate student at MIT, the fellow had talked at length about his specialty, "fiber construction," a field of study which at the time sounded esoteric and rather trivial. The notion of setting up a "textile laboratory" seemed a colossal waste of a government grant. But that was then.

Now the Rebbe asked Leibel to find the directory listing for the Massachusetts Institute of Technology, and request the textile lab. Surprisingly, instead of telling him, "You've got the wrong number," as the Rebbe had anticipated, the switchboard operator put Leibel through right away.

A youthful voice answered and Leibel asked to speak with the head of the lab. "One moment please," the student replied. "I'll see if Professor Schwartz is available." The Rebbe was delighted when he heard the name. Schwartz, he thought, must be a Jew, and that would certainly simplify things.

Eventually the Professor came on the line and the Rebbe greeted him warmly. "*Shalom aleichem*, Professor Schwartz. This is Rabbi Levi Horowitz of Brookline. I'm calling you regarding the *inyan* of *shaatnez*."

"This is Dr. Emil Schwartz," the somewhat pompous voice intoned.

Since the Professor had not reacted to the Rebbe's introduction or the reason for his call, the Rebbe concluded that Schwartz knew little about his Judaism, or at least about *shaatnez*. The Rebbe explained that he had a religious matter that concerned determining the content of fabrics and was anxious to seek the Professor's counsel.

"I'd be pleased to help in any way I can," the scientist replied, and an appointment was scheduled for the next day.

When the Rebbe arrived with several *chassidim* at the hallowed halls of MIT's textile laboratory, he was not surprised to find that there were no technicians scurrying around in white coats nor were there mice in cases, frogs cured in formaldehyde, or test tubes boiling over. Professor Schwartz received him rather ceremoniously, but without the customary greetings one Jew might exchange with another.

The Rebbe got straight down to business. First he explained the prohibition of *shaatnez* — cloth woven of wool and linen — and Schwartz readily grasped the difficulties the layman would have in detecting the presence of either fiber if they were not listed on the fabric's contents label. "By law," the Professor expounded, "the manufacturer is obliged to list the fiber contents in detail, unless the quantity of a particular fiber present is negligible, as is the case with the thread used for sewing on buttons, for example."

"That is precisely the problem," the Rebbe said. "Observant Jews are concerned about even the most minute quantities." He went on to describe the method employed to determine the presence of *shaatnez* and the problems Boston's Orthodox community had to contend with as a result of the absence of a local facility.

Dr. Schwartz's eyes lit up. "Rabbi," he exclaimed unabashedly, "you have come to the right man."

The Professor didn't exactly say that he was the world's foremost living authority on textiles and fibers, but he didn't deny it either. He detailed the government grants thus far awarded for his research, the papers he had delivered, the number of times he had lectured worldwide, and the patents he had developed to date. The list of his accomplishments was impressive, and seemingly endless.

When Schwartz paused to catch his breath, the Rebbe tried vainly to interject a word about why he had come and to steer the conversation back to the subject of *shaatnez*. But alas, he was no match for the galaxy's preeminent expert on the inner dynamics of thread. The Rebbe listened patiently to the Professor's recollections on each of the occasions he had been called upon to testify in circuit courts, before federal inquiries and Senate committees, regarding the carcinogenic qualities of various fibers. He had been the State's witness for a case in which an employee had died from the inhalation of fibers in his place of employment. The Rebbe learned Schwartz's authoritative opinion regarding future trends in fiber breakdown, his personal preferences in piece goods, and the ecological effects of the introduction of polyester. Indeed he learned everything he ever wanted to know about fabrics and their components, but had been too disinterested to ask.

Dr. Schwartz's accomplishments were mighty impressive and even mightier long, and the Rebbe fought to keep his eyes open and struggled to feign interest. Stifling a yawn, he caught a snatch of a sentence that indicated that the discussion might be heading for home base at last.

It was to his shame, the Professor diplomatically confessed, that he could not list any occasions of giving testimony before a religious court regarding *shaatnez*. In fact, he had never heard of it before the Rebbe's phone call. He now clearly considered this an egregious lacuna in his curriculum vitae, one which he was anxious to rectify, hence his keen interest in *shaatnez* research. Fully alert now, the Rebbe hung on Schwartz's every word.

The Professor related that during the course of his research he had invented a polarized microscope which highlighted the various fibers with a spectrum of colors. Under this microscope, cotton and linen, which look identical to the naked eye, appear as different hues. Thus, any fabric examined through the microscope will reveal its true colors, rendering this the ideal method of *shaatnez* detection. Schwartz assured the Rebbe that it would not be difficult for one of the Rebbe's disciples to learn how to work the wonder-microscope/*shaatnez* detector. "I would be extremely honored to teach him myself," the Professor volunteered.

The Rebbe was elated. Not only had he achieved his goal, but he had been assured — by the world's foremost authority no less — that this procedure for detecting *shaatnez* was superior to any existing method.

"How much does such a microscope cost?" the Rebbe asked innocently.

The price Schwartz quoted would have been more appropriate for an interplanetary telescope — it was astronomical! The Rebbe wondered aloud if he would be eligible for a grant to help finance this project, and Schwartz told him that he could purchase a used microscope for only a minor fortune. Somehow, the Rebbe promised himself, the money would be raised.

Before leaving the MIT lab, the Rebbe availed himself of the opportunity to satisfy his curiosity. "Professor Schwartz," he inquired, "in the course of your research have you ever discovered a detrimental side effect that might be caused by the mixture of wool and linen?" Although the Torah offers no reason for the law banning *shaatnez*, the Rebbe thought that scientific research might. "Have you ever heard of this fiber combination causing an allergic reaction or being harmful, either to the wearer or to the environment?"

Professor Schwartz removed his glasses and, with them, all of his airs of scholarship and expertise. "Rabbi," he said, speaking for once like an ordinary human being, "as of today, that is, according to the best of my knowledge and limited research, such a combination will not harm the human body or cause an adverse reaction. However, there are many things I know today that I did not know yester-day, and there are many things I will know *tomorrow* that I do not know *today*. But what I *can* say, with the fullest confidence and certainty, is that if your Bible says that the admixture is forbidden, I would place my complete trust in those sacred words."

"... *Your Bible says.*" The words rang in the Rebbe's ears. So he's not Jewish after all, the Rebbe thought to himself, chagrined. He wished more *Jews* would show such humility concerning what they know today and what they might learn tomorrow, and exhibit the profound respect this Gentile scholar had for the Holy Torah.

"Don't look so surprised, Rabbi," Dr. Schwartz went on. "Can you think of one instance when your Bible has been wrong? After years of scholarly research and scientific investigation, I, sir, cannot."

Author's note: Today the Boston religious community boasts the most sophisticated *shaatnez*-testing facility in the world.

The Case of the Footloose Firebug

"oing away for the summer" is an annual ritual with similar unpleasant associations for many people: the arduous packing, the tiresome arrangements, and — most unpleasant of all — the incessant worry about leaving the house unattended for several weeks. To allay those fears and facilitate an enjoyable vacation, neighbors are requested to keep an eye on the house, the police are asked to provide surveillance, and all windows and doors are securely locked.

As in everything else, the Chassidic Center's pre-summer vacation routine digresses from the standard. Home to hundreds of long- and short-term guests throughout the year, the Chassidic Center cannot simply close its doors after the summer solstice. The family whose father is to undergo an emergency operation at Massachusetts General cannot be expected to reschedule the surgery for the winter; the traveling businessman delayed by Friday afternoon traffic would need a place to stay for Shabbos regardless of the season; the fund-raiser compelled to abandon his family and the Land of Israel would be unable to plan his yeshiva's budget crisis for a cooler time of year. Thus when the Rebbe and his family headed for their Nantasket vacation home each summer, their house routinely remained not only unlocked, but open to total strangers.

Two nights before their departure one year, the Rebbetzin dreamt that someone had broken into the house and set it alight. This nightmare contributed its share to the family's pre-summer tension, and the Rebbetzin insisted that at the very least the guests should be asked to keep all doors and windows locked at night.

This seemingly reasonable request was quite a novel concept for the Chassidic Center, where a steady tide of comers and goers ebbs and flows twenty-four hours a day. Indeed it was a revolutionary idea, but the Rebbe was loath to deny the warning implicit in his wife's dream, and the doors of their home were locked for the first time. The guests were informed of the new procedure and duplicate keys were distributed.

This done, the Rebbetzin was able to relax and the family departed on schedule for their summer vacation. This much-needed leisure time, however, was not meant to be.

At 5:00 A.M. the following morning, the Rebbe's family was awakened by the police with the news that there had been a fire at the Chassidic Center. The officer asked the Rebbe to return to Brookline at once to help with the investigation.

"Investigation?" the Rebbe asked.

"That's right," the patrolman replied. "They suspect it

was arson. But don't worry, Rabbi. They don't think you done it — you wasn't even there."

The Rebbe was aghast. The image of a charred, gutted Chassidic Center registered in his mind and made him shudder with anxiety. The Rebbetzin's nightmare had become a reality.

Sixteen hours after their arrival in Nantasket, the family returned home to assess the damage and take steps to replace the roof over their, and many other, heads. The pervasive, heart-stopping stench of smoke struck them well before the Chassidic Center came into view. It was therefore with great relief that they found the building standing, instead of a smoking ruins.

The Chassidic Center had in fact suffered only light damage, but the *shul* was partially destroyed. A burnt crisp was all that remained of the *shulchan*; there was no *zecher* of the *mechitzah*. The *aron kodesh* had been hosed down and was mostly intact, although the *sifrei Torah* were somewhat soggy. Fortunately the fire had not spread to any other part of the building.

After a thorough inspection, the Rebbetzin phoned their insurance company. The repairs would be costly and the premises had to be rehabilitated as quickly as possible. To the Rebbe's consternation, he was informed that before an assessor could be sent to estimate the extent of the damage and evaluate the claim, the insurance company had to speak to the Fire Department.

Later that afternoon, the insurance agent called back to say that dispatching an assessor and all other matters relating to the Chassidic Center's coverage had been placed on hold while the police investigation was under way. That was the second worst piece of news the Rebbe had heard that day.

The last thing anyone wanted was an investigation of the Chassidic Center, even if it was only for the purpose of determining how the fire had started. The Rebbe of course had nothing to hide, but experience had taught him that an investigation always meant media coverage, and media coverage always meant a newsworthy item, and a newsworthy item always meant a sensational scoop uncovered or, if necessary, created.

Some congregants who were sifting through the scorched remains of the *shul* seemed better-informed about the arson investigation. According to them, not only had the Fire Marshal not discovered any natural cause for the fire, but all of the telltale signs of arson were present, including a mangled, blackened gasoline can which had been found among the ashes. The police were convinced that it was an inside job: the doors and windows had all been locked and there was no evidence of forced entry.

Since an investigation was inevitable, the Rebbe tried to devise a way to minimize its detrimental effect on the community as a whole and on the Chassidic Center in particular. He suggested to the Rebbetzin that they consider each of their guests to determine who among them could be eliminated as a possible culprit.

The Rebbetzin was appalled. "You don't think that one of our boarders actually set fire to the *shul*, do you?"

"Of course not," the Rebbe replied, "but the police do, and I would like to expedite their investigation. The sooner they apprehend the perpetrator, the sooner we can collect our insurance and renovate the building."

Nodding her agreement, the Rebbetzin took a pad of paper and began to list the boarders. There was Jeff, the Boston University graduate student; the two *meshulachim* from *Eretz Yisrael*, one from *Yerushalayim* and the other from Bnei Brak; the Feldblums, whose daughter was to undergo surgery; and of course, Leibel.

The very mention of Leibel's name in the context of arson sent the Horowitzes, despite the gravity of the situation, into paroxysms of laughter. Leibel, it was well-known, had a pathological fear of fires. As a matter of fact, he had a pathological fear of dogs, insects, lightning, the dark, the police, and the common cold, to name but a few of his phobias. Not for a moment did anyone ever doubt that the most unqualified man on earth had been hired to serve as security officer of the Chassidic Center. But among his countless apprehensions and anxieties, pyrophobia was the greatest of all.

The Rebbe explained that, according to police procedure, in order for an individual to qualify as a suspect, he would need to have a motive for committing the crime, the opportunity to do so, and the means to carry it out. Clearly each guest had the "opportunity" to set the fire, but none of them had an obvious "motive." In the case of arson, however, the motive might be less obvious than for other crimes: a harbored resentment, perhaps, or — since a *shul* was involved — anti-Semitism; or the arsonist might simply be a person suffering from an emotional disorder.

It was highly unlikely that any of these motives applied to the Feldblums, who had come to the Chassidic Center only a few days earlier — without any advance notice — for emergency medical treatment. Their daughter had a brain tumor which had grown so large that it had fractured her skull. That people in such a situation would even contemplate arson — particularly of the building which provided them shelter — was unthinkable.

The two fund-raisers from Israel were no strangers to the Rebbe. They had stayed at the Chassidic Center on their previous visits and were exceptionally fine, scholarly gentlemen who had come to America for one purpose only. As soon as they raised enough money to marry off their children, they would return home. They too had nothing to gain by setting fire to the base of their New England activities.

Leibel, unquestionably, was absolutely above suspicion.

That left Jeff, a religious B.U. grad student in applied mathematics. He had moved into the Chassidic Center to distance himself from the college campus environment, and hopefully to enhance his chances of finding the right girl. The Rebbe thought for a moment about a possible motive. "Maybe Jeff is frustrated over his studies?" he suggested.

The Rebbetzin quickly came to the young man's defense. "Jeff probably hasn't had trouble with his studies since the day he started kindergarten," she said, actually understating the case. Jeff's mind was like a computer from the year 3000. "I wonder if his professors can keep up with him."

"Perhaps he received a 'Dear John' letter from the girl he's been seeing?" the Rebbe offered.

"Why do we have to guess," the Rebbetzin replied, "when we can ask him directly?"

Jeff, they discovered, was terribly distressed over the fire.

Indeed it was the only time the Rebbe recalled seeing the young man that he didn't appear to be doing advanced calculus differentials in his head. The Rebbe asked him to tell them everything that had happened the previous night.

"I had just fallen asleep, when the fire broke out," Jeff related. It was only an hour after he'd returned home from a late date with his young lady, a thought which brought a broad smile to his serious face. The Rebbetzin mentally crossed the "Dear John" letter off her motive list and gave the Rebbe a knowing look.

"When I came to the house and tried to open the downstairs door," Jeff continued, "I found it was locked. Then I remembered the Rebbetzin's new policy of keeping the place closed at night, and realized I had left my new key in my other jacket. I had no recourse but to knock loudly on the door until someone let me in.

"Eventually Mrs. Feldblum opened up for me. I went upstairs, thought for a while about the evening's developments, and then prepared for bed. The next thing I knew someone was yelling for all of us to evacuate the building and there was a tremendous commotion in the hallway. Downstairs, there was smoke everywhere, and the firemen were hosing everything in sight. It was horrible. Thank God, the fire didn't spread beyond the *shul*."

"It's a good thing the windows and doors were closed," the Rebbetzin interjected. "That probably helped to contain the fire."

"Maybe so," the Rebbe added, "but it seems the firemen decided to soak the upper stories of the building anyway, just for good measure."

"Soaked is right," Jeff remarked, shaking his head from side to side. "My notebooks have been reduced to a clotted mass of waterlogged logarithms!"

Jeff's story removed any suspicions the Rebbe might have entertained about his complicity in the crime. As soon as he finished his rendition, Leibel Wattstein strutted into the house. Remarkably Leibel seemed to have weathered the storm well; he actually appeared none the worse for his exposure to the fire. In fact, he was in amazingly good spirits for a so-called security man who had failed not only to protect the premises but to apprehend the perpetrator.

The Rebbetzin reached instinctively for one of Leibel's favorite *noshes*, and placed it in front of him to encourage him to speak. Leibel really needed little encouragement, looking as if he were bursting to recount his epic heroism, but he helped himself to several servings all the same. His version of the night's proceedings differed somewhat from Jeff's.

"I was innocently sleeping in my bed," Leibel began as he polished off the last of the Rebbetzin's apple pie, "as any law-abiding citizen should during the night, when all of a sudden I felt myself under attack. I didn't want to hurt the intruders, so I pulled the covers tightly over my head. I hoped that after a few minutes they would leave me alone, or else I'd have to get rough with them! Even for a man with a kind disposition like me," Leibel continued, "there's just so long that I can be 'Mr. Nice Guy.'

"But they ignored my peaceful overtures. Soon I was surrounded by these men in white who started fooling around with my face! I pretended to be asleep but I peeked out at them with my eyes half-closed. You should have seen them, Rebbe — I think they were Martians! The Whities began to fight among themselves over who would have me: one grabbed my arm, the other went for my head, and the third one played with the controls on a weird black box he had, trying to lure me to him, I guess.

"The one who was after my head insisted that I was his, and to prove his point, he put this big black mask over my nose and mouth so that I would be forced to inhale a secret potion. I fought him off with all my might, but somehow the three of them managed to overpower me. Once they had me in their clutches, they strapped me into the space module and turned on their anti-radar lights, and we began to soar into outer space. Hundreds of G-forces were tugging at me as we left the Earth's gravitational pull, but since I'm in such great shape, I was able to withstand it.

"As we screeched into orbit, the lights began to flash brighter and rotate in a frenzy. We neared their planet. Sirens began to scream, wail and howl as we circled their headquarters. Obviously they decided that a catch like me had to go straight to their leader, so they landed right outside his palace. A big commotion was going on and other Whities surrounded us to rush me in to their Great One's chambers."

The Rebbe understood that a good part of Leibel's fantasy had been conjured up so as to avoid the admission that, instead of guarding the premises as he was supposed to, Leibel had slept right through the fire. Indeed since he *had* slept through the pandemonium and intense heat, the fire fighters had been convinced that Leibel was suffering from smoke inhalation, and an ambulance had been called. When the "Whities," or, as they are known in common jargon, the paramedics, had tried to revive him with oxygen, and Leibel had stubbornly continued to feign unconsciousness, they rushed him to the hospital in their "space module," where the Great One had apparently judged him fit for intergalactic travel and released him. Leibel had made his way home on foot.

Although it was clear to the Rebbe that no one from the Chassidic Center could have started the fire, it was not so clear to the Police Department. They were very anxious to begin their investigation, and the Rebbe could no longer delay them without appearing suspect. To his distress, he discovered that the police had no intention of conducting their investigation beyond the walls of the Chassidic Center: they were certain the culprit was to be found among the residents.

Detectives Gallagher and MacLachlan, two of Boston's Finest, briefed the Rebbe on their suspicions that the arson had been an inside job.

"We can eliminate you and your wife from the list of possible perpetrators," MacLachlan said, glancing down at his note pad as Gallagher nodded his agreement, "since neither of you was here at the time of the fire. Whoever was will have to be interrogated." Both detectives licked the ends of their pencils, poised to write.

The Rebbe proceeded to name all those who were present, and at the same time explain why he felt that each could not be guilty of arson, but the policemen were unimpressed with his reasoning; the Rebbetzin was unimpressed with the cops. "You're wasting your time looking here for the criminal," she told them. "You should be out on the street, talking to witnesses and finding clues!"

Gallagher and MacLachlan dismissed her advice with the comment that their years on the force had rendered them proficient at apprehending criminals. They were adequately trained and highly qualified to proceed with their work the way they knew best.

The Rebbetzin was forced to concede that she did not possess such credentials, and she sat down to read the morning paper.

The Rebbe described Mr. and Mrs. Feldblum and assured the police that they were not the perpetrators; he gave some background information about the *meshulachim* and explained that they had absolutely nothing to gain from the crime.

"We'll draw our own conclusions, Rabbi," the detectives countered.

Then the Rebbe told them about his good old friend Leibel.

"Who's he?" they asked.

Twenty years of history scrolled through the Rebbe's mind as he searched for whatever might be relevant to the investigation. "He is a geriatric loner whom my father picked up off the street," the Rebbe said. "He has no family and few friends; this is his home. You might say he's an old family retainer. He does odd jobs, occasionally cleans up the building, and loafs extensively. And there is no doubt whatsoever," the Rebbe added with a note of finality, "that this man is innocent."

Gallagher perked up. "How can you be so sure?" he asked.

Trying to keep a straight face, the Rebbe replied, "Leibel

is no pyromaniac. In fact you might say he is a pyropho-
biac." The Rebbe gave an abbreviated rendition of Leibel's activities during the fire, judiciously omitting any
mention of Martians or spaceships.

The cops both rolled their eyes, as if to say, "This is
evidence?" and made copious notations on their pads.

"Anybody else?" Gallagher asked, and the Rebbe told
them about Jeff, the graduate student, and where he was
on the night of the fire.

"He was out the entire night on a date?" MacLachlan
asked incredulously.

"No," the Rebbe replied, "he returned at two-thirty."
The cops exchanged glances and wrote feverishly.

"Let's see this Jeff first," they said in unison.

The Rebbe was about to send for him when the Rebbetzin intervened. "Hold your horses!" she blurted out
abruptly. "You can call off your investigation. I know who
did it." Her words were met with a stunned silence.

"I know who set fire to our house," she repeated. "Roy
Gianetti did it. This guy." The Rebbetzin pointed excitedly
to the picture of the Lowell arsonist prominently displayed
on the front page of her newspaper.

Barely according the photo a glance, the policemen
groaned with exasperation. "Lady," MacLachlan said
gruffly, "d'ya mind if we handle this?"

"I'm only trying to do my civic duty," the Rebbetzin
protested. "We've already told you that the arsonist cannot
possibly be one of our guests. Why do you have to waste
your time and our tax dollars interviewing innocent people when Gianetti's already behind bars. If you don't
believe me, go speak to him yourself — you've got him in

police custody."

"With all due respect," Gallagher replied in a tone that indicated his patience was wearing thin, "just because you read about the apprehension of a firebug in Lowell, it doesn't mean that he set fire to this here building in Brookline."

"If you'd only finish reading the article," MacLachlan added, "you'd see that all of Gianetti's fires were in Lowell, not over here."

"I've never noticed a Berlin Wall separating the neighborhoods," the Rebbetzin parried, "and if my eyes don't deceive me, he's not wearing a pair of cement shoes in this picture. Maybe he jogged over."

"You're missing the point, lady," Gallagher stubbornly insisted. "According to our report this here joint was locked at the time of the fire, so even if your boy-wonder arsonist could get from Lowell to Brookline, how'd he get in here when there were no signs of a break-in?"

"I'm sure there's a simple explanation," the Rebbetzin asserted with great assurance. "Probably, when Mrs. Feldblum let Jeff in after his date, she forgot to lock the front door. Later on she remembered that the door was open so she came down again and locked it. I do that kind of thing all the time."

"That makes as much sense," Gallagher exclaimed, "as...." All eyes focused on the detective as his audience avidly awaited the end of this analogy, but it just hung in midsentence until finally he tapped his index finger against his temple.

"Well said, Officer," the Rebbetzin commented drily, and resumed her attack. "Now would you mind getting on with solving this crime?"

"That's exactly what we're trying to do," MacLachlan retorted indignantly. "You gotta face it, this was an inside job, and this grad student of yours seems to be a very likely suspect. You've been in Boston probably as long as we have, so I don't have to tell you that college students do crazy things."

The Rebbe saw the logic of that argument, but the Rebbetzin would not budge. "Crazy, perhaps, but self-destructive? Never! Why would a Phi Beta Kappa honor student set fire to a building and then go to sleep two floors above the blaze? Besides, he's short — that's why he's still dating."

The Rebbetzin had seized the initiative and was making good progress, until she dropped that final non sequitur. Gallagher looked at MacLachlan, MacLachlan looked at the Rebbe, and the Rebbe looked at the Rebbetzin, each of them shrugging their shoulders in bafflement at the significance of the height factor.

It took the Rebbetzin a moment to perceive what it was that the others had not perceived, and she went on to explain that she had found a very large footprint in her flowerbed. "It could only have been the footprint of someone big and tall, certainly not Jeff — he's only 5'4" or so." She then read a line from the newspaper article which said that Roy Gianetti was six feet, six inches tall!

"Gentlemen," she concluded, "*your* firebug is *our* firebug. So maybe you would be kind enough to help us collect our insurance now?"

While the detectives conceded that there might be something to what the Rebbetzin had said, it was still refuted by their original claim that the arsonist lived and carried out his "calling" in Lowell. The Rebbetzin, however, would not relent.

"It looks to me like he's got a fine pair of thumbs," she persisted, hooking one of hers in an exaggerated demonstration of hitchhiker body English, "and I'm sure you officers have heard of public transportation — you know, one of the conveniences of the automotive age. We are a mobile society, after all, and even a seven-footer can fit into a streetcar."

By this time the Rebbetzin had commandeered the discussion and she was about to give the officers another excoriation about squandering tax dollars when the detectives explained that since Gianetti had been arrested and was being held in a different district, they were not authorized to interrogate him.

Before responding, the Rebbetzin scrutinized them closely, checking for signs of latent dementia. Unable to detect any overt symptoms, she said simply, "Don't worry about a thing. I'm sure the Rabbi will be able to arrange something for you — he's got a few connections," and she made as if to dial the Rebbe's police liaison.

To save face, MacLachlan agreed to look into the matter, but the Rebbetzin had a few more suggestions for him. "From what I've heard," she said, "arsonists like to brag. I'm sure you won't have any trouble getting Gianetti to talk. Also, take a good look at the photographs that the Police Department took during the fire."

"Photographs?" the Rebbe asked.

"Sure, you know — the pictures! Arsonists not only like to brag, they also get perverse pleasure from watching their handiwork in action. I read somewhere that the authorities always take pictures of the crowds that gather to watch a fire, to see if a familiar face appears. I'm sure that's how they caught the Lowell arsonist, although they'd never write that in the press. They couldn't miss spotting a giant like Gianetti."

"Okay, all right," MacLachlan said, reassuming command. Now that he knew what to do, he didn't want it to appear as though he had just been enlightened. "We'll check our pictures and if we find anything, we'll arrange an interview with the Lowell arsonist." He replaced his pencil in his pocket and flipped his note pad shut. "But if Gianetti isn't implicated," he added ominously, "we'll be back to interrogate every resident that was present on the night of the fire, and we'll expect your full cooperation." With those words Gallagher and MacLachlan swaggered out the door.

Despite his faith in the Rebbetzin's intuition and clarity of thought, the Rebbe was still nervous. To his astonishment, however, his wife was the essence of tranquillity. How could she have blocked the arson or the impending police investigation out of her mind? he wondered.

"There's nothing to worry about," she asserted nonchalantly.

"Nothing to worry about?!" the Rebbe repeated. "Why, you know as well as I do what kind of negative publicity a police probe could bring to the Chassidic Center!"

"There is nothing to worry about," she explained,

"because the case is closed."

And indeed it was.

THE NEXT MORNING Detectives Gallagher and MacLachlan returned with two empty bottles of schnapps and the news that they had found the perpetrator, none other than Roy Gianetti. "Your wife was right on the mark," Gallagher began. "He was in the pictures, loves to brag, came in when she reckoned — the works," and he proceeded to tell the story:

"Gianetti, recently dubbed the Tenement Torch, started all his fires in the vicinity of his old boarding school. He must have had a pretty miserable time there, 'cause he burned it down and then started his own personal urban renewal program by burning down one old rat-trap after another in the neighborhood. Apparently, he really hated the house mother, so he decided to set fire to her home as well. Since she lived in Brookline, he hitchhiked, took a trolley and walked the rest of the way — just like the Missus said. But it was believed that that fire was of natural origin, so no one connected it with yours. Anyway, by the time Gianetti got that fire going, he was exhausted, and went down Beacon Street looking for a place to crash."

"When he came to the grocery across from your home," MacLachlan continued, picking up where his partner had left off, "he saw a sign pointing to the Episcopalian Church directly behind this place. Gianetti is Catholic and not especially religious, but he reasoned that any church was good for free lodging, even if he had to break in to get it.

"But Gianetti mistook this place for the Episcopalian

Church* and walked right in the front door which was unlocked at the time." The Rebbetzin merely smiled. "He went straight to the sanctuary," the detective went on, "where he found a couple of bottles of liquor, and drank himself to sleep."

The bottles, the Rebbe recalled at once, were left over from a *kiddush* in honor of his oldest daughter's marriage. MacLachlan and Gallagher resumed their Huntley-Brinkley act, taking turns relating the sequence of events of that fateful night, each and every detail bearing out the Rebbetzin's analysis:

Later that night, when Mrs. Feldblum had come back down to lock the door, she inadvertently awoke the arsonist who had been sleeping in the *shul.* Irritated at being disturbed, Gianetti arose, only to discover that he was not in a church but in a synagogue. It didn't take him long to remember that his hatred for Jews was as great as his hatred for the house mother, and he seized the opportunity to express it. Thanks to the Rebbetzin's new policy of keeping all the doors and windows closed, together with a mighty helping of Divine Assistance, the fire remained localized and did not consume the entire building.

Roy Gianetti fled the scene of the crime but briefly, and minutes later commingled with the small group of late-

---

* Gianetti was not the only one ever to make that mistake, as the Church served a special clientele: the deaf and dumb. It was not uncommon for one or two of them to wander into the *shul* during *Shacharis* on Sunday mornings. Due to the parishioners' handicap, however, their services never disturbed the Chassidic Center, nor did the goings-on at the Chassidic Center ever bother the Church-goers.

night spectators who had gathered to witness the event. Obviously a six-foot-six-incher doesn't mingle unobtrusively, and he was easily identified in the photos.

Just as the Rebbetzin had predicted, Gianetti was filled with hubris over his accomplishments and was not at all reticent in boasting about them. The Lowell police discounted the entire story as unadulterated fiction, and attributed his verbal meanderings to typical criminal vainglory. Gianetti went on the defensive and produced as evidence that he had set fire to the Chassidic Center two empty schnapps bottles which he had purloined and stashed as souvenirs.

The bottles, after forensic examination, had been released and the cops had come back to return them to the Rebbe and to tip their hats to the Rebbetzin for her outstanding detective work.

"We'll give you a letter confirming that the investigation is closed," MacLachlan told her, "and you can have the insurance company send their man down. Then, I suppose, you can get back to Nantasket and finish your vacation."

"Thank you, gentlemen," the Rebbe said, "but I doubt that we'll be rushing off now — it's the Fourth of July weekend and the roads will be impossible."

Gallagher looked at MacLachlan, and MacLachlan looked at Gallagher. "No sweat, Rabbi," they chimed, their timing precise. "We'll provide a police escort."

AS THE REBBE'S DRIVER floored the accelerator to keep pace with their "escort," the Rebbe eyed the speedometer anxiously. The squad car's blaring siren and flashing lights blazed a trail through the holiday traffic, and the sound-and-light show was impressive indeed.

"I can see why Leibel thought he'd been launched into outer space," the Rebbetzin remarked.

"Yes," the Rebbe agreed, "but I sincerely hope these Whities aren't leading us straight to the Great One!"

Day of Judgment

G ood Shabbos!" Dr. Himmelstein boomed heartily to all and sundry.

"G…g…good Shabbos," the Rebbe responded, trying to find his voice. Yosef Aaron Himmelstein's presence, not to mention his demeanor, had taken the Rebbe completely by surprise. A pillar of the community, the retired Professor of metallurgy was one of the most affable and generous individuals to grace New England, and it certainly was not unusual for him to wish everyone a "Good Shabbos" in his stentorian voice. Nor was it unusual for the most happy-go-lucky fellow the Rebbe had ever met to be indulging in shmaltz herring while admonishing everyone about the detrimental effects of ingesting mercury, excessive levels of which were present in locally processed fish. The man always had a ready quip or an anecdote to tell, and an infectious spirit that could uplift even the most cheerless situation. In spite of this, the Rebbe was surprised to see him in his usual jocular mood; indeed he was surprised to see him in *shul* altogether!

The previous Thursday, Himmelstein had been indicted on several counts of grand larceny and fraud. According to the local papers, it was one of the biggest investment swindles of the year, and Himmelstein's arrest and subsequent release on bail were the talk of the town.

Frankly, it was hard to believe that Dr. Himmelstein — a man as honest as he was well-loved, as earnest as he was kind, as forthright as he was friendly — might be guilty. But somehow the Rebbe would have expected a man whose name had been broadcast over the airwaves nonstop, and whose sterling reputation had been severely tarnished, to adopt a somewhat lower profile. Anxious to hear the inside story, the Rebbe invited Yosef Aaron over to his study for a chat, and he readily accepted.

In the relative privacy of his home, the Rebbe told Himmelstein that while he was relieved to see the Professor looking so cheerful, he was deeply concerned.

"Whatever for?" Himmelstein asked with complete candor.

"Well, the papers...," the Rebbe muttered, "the indictment...."

"Oh, *that*," Himmelstein responded, dismissing the entire matter with a flick of his wrist.

"Yosef Aaron," the Rebbe said gravely, "this is no laughing matter. Aside from the damage the accusations can cause to your and your children's reputations, there is talk of a hefty jail sentence!" But his words had no effect on Yosef Aaron's high spirits.

"Don't worry, Rebbe," he replied lightly.

"My dear Professor," the Rebbe said, "you've told me nothing which might alleviate my worrying. I reiterate: I am very concerned!"

Seeing the Rebbe's distress and his agitated state, Dr. Himmelstein raised both his hands defensively, as if to indicate that although he considered it unnecessary, he would nevertheless reveal why he was so unperturbed. The Rebbe waited anxiously to hear his explanation but all he offered was, "I'm innocent. It's as simple as that."

"I have no doubt about it," the Rebbe assured him, implying that such a statement was not sufficient to dispel anxiety.

"Rebbe, I'm innocent," he repeated, "and I know that God will look after me in my hour of need."

"My friend," the Rebbe countered, "you know that you don't have to convince me of the value of *bitachon*. I too am certain that the Almighty will come to your aid, but that does not preclude our taking some precautions which will invite Divine Assistance. We must be practical," he counseled. "We are not dealing with the Sanhedrin, but with American civil law, and one may not have too much confidence in this system. Many an innocent man has been convicted of a crime he did not commit. Guiltless individuals have served prison sentences under the sanction of due process and statutory jurisprudence. Do you have any proof of your innocence?"

"You mean aside from the fact that the police have caught the felon?"

"What felon is that?"

"The felon who stole my stationery." Realizing that the Rebbe's knowledge of the case was incomplete, Himmelstein began to relate the entire episode from the beginning:

"Early last week," he said, "the BPD Bunco Squad completed its investigation into a fraudulent investment scheme involving scores of local citizens, notably, the residents of the New England Retirement Village, among others. It seems that these people received literature outlining a newly patented, cost-effective procedure for extracting copper ore from slag. You see, Rebbe, in the refining process, the valuable metal is separated from the impurities. Residual quantities of ore remain in the fused dross after smelting, but to extract these minute amounts has always proved impractical: the process is more costly than the residue is worth at current market prices.

"In any event, a letter accompanying this literature, on my stationery, signed, presumably, by me and detailing my credentials as former chairman of the Department of Metallurgy at MIT, urged the addressees to invest sums of money from $5,000 and up in the development of the new process, to get in on the ground floor, so to speak, of a once-in-a-lifetime opportunity to strike it rich. Among those who succumbed to the temptation were faculty members — ex-colleagues of mine — and senior citizens who could ill afford the loss. Outraged — and rightfully so — the victims lodged complaints with the police, and I was arrested.

"The very same day I was indicted, the cops arrested a young felon by the name of Willie Jones for a different crime, and found several sheets of my letterhead in his possession. He was employed by the university as a cleaning boy and among his responsibilities were the offices and labs in the metallurgy department. He confessed to having swiped the stationery from a cabinet in my old office."

As soon as Himmelstein mentioned this last detail, the Rebbe understood why his friend was at ease, but he was still perplexed. "If they've caught the thief," the Rebbe asked, "and he admits having stolen your stationery, why have you only been released on your own recognizance? Why weren't the charges against you dropped?"

"Good question, Rebbe. I asked it myself. Apparently the prosecution thinks that Jones's testimony is inconclusive. There's nothing tying him to the investment scam. I believe he was only a small cog in a much bigger wheel."

The Rebbe's spirits sank. He pondered for a moment and then asked, "If, as you say, these criminals arranged for the theft of your stationery, how did they get your John Hancock?"

"It's not as difficult as you might think to copy someone's signature," Himmelstein replied. "It would be a simple matter for someone in a maintenance worker's uniform, who is already engaged in emptying wastebaskets, to retrieve discarded credit card receipts from the university bookstore, which I still frequent. Anyone familiar with my routine would know that, and know I charge my purchases. But it's *not* my signature they duplicated."

Dr. Himmelstein then related a story about the famous Rabbi Naftali Tzvi Yehuda Berlin, better known by his acronym, the *Netziv*. That towering *Rosh Yeshiva* of Volozhin was accustomed to signing his full name with a tiny apostrophe between the two *yuds* of Tzvi and Yehuda, since the juxtaposition of these two letters form *Hashem*'s name.

Once, the *maskilim*, the so-called "Enlightenists," accused the *Netziv* of having minted counterfeit money. The evidence they presented was a document which he had allegedly signed to that effect. The signature was indeed in the *Netziv*'s handwriting, but he was able to disprove the claim by pointing out that the apostrophe he always inserted between the *yuds* in his name was absent in the forgery.

"Ever since I heard that story," Himmelstein said, "I adopted the custom of inserting an apostrophe — it's really no more than a tiny hairline — between my first two initials and my last name, because I sign my name YA Himmelstein, and the Y and the A together with the H of Himmelstein form the name of God.

"The bogus signature on the letter to potential investors does not have the small line between the YA and the H ...."

"Wonderful!" the Rebbe exclaimed, his spirits soaring like heated mercury. Dr. Himmelstein, however, was quick to cool him down. He reminded the Rebbe that he had only adopted this custom of late; he had sixty years of signatures, including the one on his driver's license, with no apostrophe separating the YA and the H. His lawyer had advised him not even to mention this point in court because it would lose him more credibility than it could possibly gain.

That was not significant; what mattered was that when the Rebbe heard this, he became thoroughly convinced of Himmelstein's innocence and thoroughly committed to doing all that he could to bring about Yosef Aaron's exoneration.

A few days after the Rebbe's meeting with Himmelstein, the assistant District Attorney of Boston, Mr. Robert Ashe, requested an interview, and the Rebbe quickly acceded to his request. Yosef Aaron had already informed the Rebbe that Ashe was out for blood: the District Attorney was retiring at the end of his term and would not be standing for reelection; his assistant considered himself a most worthy successor. Ashe was under close scrutiny for the post and an inability to land a conviction in this well-publicized case could jeopardize his nomination.

Himmelstein's lawyer, Sidney Levinson, with whom the Rebbe had spoken twice since his "Shabbos briefing," confirmed Yosef Aaron's suspicions and asserted that Ashe was working overtime on the case in his attempt to get everything tied up in a neat little package. Levinson told the Rebbe that he had tried to reason with Ashe but the assistant D.A. was thoroughly disinterested in seeking truth; all he wanted was a feather in his cap. A major fraud case was just the kind of prosecution Ashe had been hoping for and he wasn't about to abandon it over a minor detail like possibly convicting an innocent man.

Robert Ashe, Esq. arrived precisely on schedule and parked across the street from the Chassidic Center. He asked the Rebbe a battery of questions about Himmelstein's character and kept trying to twist the Rebbe's unwavering answers about the Professor's gilt-edged integrity to suit his own needs. During the course of the interview he asked the Rebbe if he had noticed Himmelstein's flashy life style.

"That is simply the way he lives," the Rebbe replied. "He is generous with others and apparently enjoys certain comforts himself."

To this Ashe countered that people had told him Himmelstein had not been like this five years earlier. The implication was obvious. The Rebbe explained that Yosef Aaron had indeed had a financial setback about five years ago and for a time he had led a more modest life. "But I have known Dr. Himmelstein for many years," the Rebbe said. "Perhaps you might want to verify what I've told you with others who are better acquainted with the Professor. I'm sure they would confirm that he and his family have always lived well."

"As of very recently there have been visible signs of a significant increase in Dr. Himmelstein's assets," the assistant D.A. claimed. "Strange, wouldn't you say, for a professor to become more affluent after he retires? You didn't happen to notice his new car, did you?"

The Rebbe responded by asking if the late-model Oldsmobile across the street belonged to Ashe. The assistant D.A. engaged in some embarrassed throat-clearing and the Rebbe diplomatically changed the subject. He pointed out that nowhere in their discussion had Ashe used the term "alleged." "Mr. Ashe, you do believe a man is innocent until proven guilty, don't you?"

Ashe offered his shallow acquiescence. "I understand," the Rebbe continued, "that the defendant claims he is innocent. He says that sheets of his letterhead were stolen, and that the thief has been apprehended and has admitted the crime. Aren't these adequate grounds for dismissing the charges?"

From the pen of
Hanoch Teller

The Bostoner
Stories and Recollections from the Colorful Chassidic Court of the Bostoner Rebbe

Unique among chassidic leaders in his ability to relate to the American milieu, Rabbi Levi I. Horowitz has earned the unreserved praise of the Jewish people for his outstanding achievements. With the flair for humor and drama that has made Hanoch Teller the contemporary king of storytelling, he retells the Rebbe's extraordinary stories.

Pichifkes
Stories Heard On the Road and By the Way

This globe-trotting author and lecturer hears new, inspiring stories wherever he goes. In Vienna, Hong Kong, New Orleans, Melbourne, Jerusalem, Riga or Calgary, Jews seek him out to relate their fascinating experiences. Hanoch Teller offers his own unique rendition of them, retold in his masterful and entertaining "soul style."

Courtrooms of the Mind
Stories and Advice on Judging Others Favorably

The Torah enjoins us to judge our fellow man favorably, and to ask ourselves: has he indeed erred, or have *we*, in evaluating the evidence? These two-books-in-one (for adults and for children) present 20 actual cases tried in the courtrooms of the mind, where the only defense witnesses are the heart and soul.

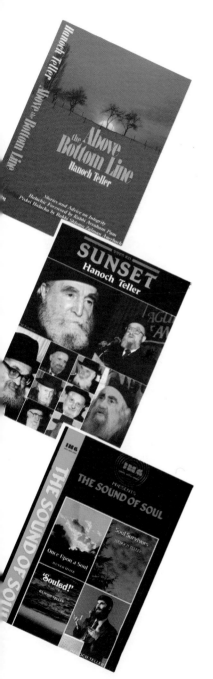

Above the Bottom Line
Stories and Advice on Integrity

Integrity is one of the most difficult attributes to acquire, and one of the easiest to lose. Temptations abound, and the "bottom line"—the net profit in any transaction—blinds our conscience to more important considerations. These amusing, provocative, and often searing stories heighten our awareness of G-d's aversion to deception, and teach us to rise above expediency. With a halachic foreword by Rabbi Avraham Pam and *piskei halacha* by Rabbi Shlomo Zalman Auerbach.

Sunset
Stories of Our Contemporary Torah Luminaries and their Spiritual Heroism

Instructive and dramatic episodes in the lives of ten contemporary Torah luminaries, including Hagaon Harav Moshe Feinstein and the Steipler Gaon, *zt"l*. These inspiring stories of spiritual heroism will teach and touch generations to come.

The Sound of Soul I
The Sound of Soul II

A special selection of Hanoch Teller masterpieces, written and adapted for audio transmission in collaboration with Marsi Tabak, is now available on cassette. Fully dramatized and narrated by Reuven Dovid Miller, these inspiring tapes guarantee hours of listening pleasure.

Once Upon a Soul

A veritable celebration of Jewish survival, these twenty-five powerful true stories fascinate, embolden and enrich, expressing the deepest truths of the human soul. Heartwarming, enlightening, poignant tales to uplift the spirit.

Soul Survivors

In this collection of amazing, true stories, as in life itself, the mighty hand of G-d reaches out to His faithful wherever they may be: in a speeding Detroit taxi, a goatskin tent, or a tank under fire. Two dozen more gems in Hanoch Teller's glittering treasure trove of contemporary Jewish literature.

'Souled!'

"Soul stories" for the entire family! Adults will savor Book I's tales of altruism, salvation, serendipity, and nobility, while children will be edified and entertained by Book II's legends and lore. Hilarity, pathos, drama and irony combine for a brilliant finale to the soul trilogy.

Bridges of Steel, Ladders of Gold
Joseph Tanenbaum: Builder of Bridges to Torah

The rags-to-riches story of the philanthropist-par-excellence who turned heavy industry on its head with cost-cutting strategies that left him a millionaire. Now this enterprising octogenarian endows hundreds of Torah institutions, building bridges between the assimilated and their proud heritage.

The assistant D.A. dismissed the Rebbe's argument instead. "The testimony of this thief is as reliable as the testimony of a convicted perjurer. He was under the influence of narcotics at the time he made the confession and he didn't know what he was saying or why he was saying it. Obviously he thought that saying he had stolen the stationery would clear him of the crime he'd been caught perpetrating.

"I have personally prosecuted Willie Jones three times in his, shall we say, colorful career," Ashe went on to say. "The kid's only nineteen years old and he's already been busted eleven times (although never convicted). Believe me, his word is meaningless. Your Dr. Himmelstein is the big fish in this operation, and I'm going to hook him!"

The Rebbe could see that Ashe refused to relate to anything which might diminish his chances of securing a conviction. What he'd said about Jones's reliability made sense, but the Rebbe felt Ashe was not in the least interested in pursuing *any* possibility of Himmelstein's innocence. Himmelstein's and his lawyer's assessment of the man's ambitiousness had apparently been accurate.

THE VENOM which Ashe had displayed in the Rebbe's house was but a foretaste of his presentation in court. He had amassed a mind-boggling array of questionable evidence which he delivered as though it were unimpeachable. He deftly manipulated the thoughts of the jury members; it seemed it would be impossible for Levinson to undo the damage.

In his opening argument, Ashe, with his thumbs hooked arrogantly in his vest, strutted around the courtroom like a bad actor in a theatrical performance. He paused dramatically at the judge's bench and at the windows as he revealed each new detail about the Machiavellian character of "the venal Dr. Himmelstein." The effect of his peregrinations on the jury was astounding.

Gliding his hand down the railing of the jury box, staring each juror in the eye, the prosecutor harangued, "Before you sits a successful, affluent man, exuding power and respectability, who enjoys the admiration and adulation of his community. Where did this power and respect come from? My learned colleague, Mr. Levinson, will attempt to prove he earned it, but the prosecution will demonstrate unequivocably that he *bought* it — with tainted money!

"With magnanimous donations and impressive gifts he purchased the respect and insured the silence of anyone who might have protested his despicable ways. This man is an embarrassment to the world of academia, a disgrace to the scientific community, and a nemesis to public morality. He has secured his lofty position in society by enticing unsuspecting senior citizens to invest their life savings in a get-rich-quick scheme, bilking the elderly of their meager social security funds, mercilessly reducing them to penury.

"Ladies and gentlemen of the jury, I submit that Dr. Joseph Himmelstein has indeed not retired; he has simply embarked on a new career. Instead of devoting himself to enriching lives through education, he now works full time at *destroying* lives, reaping enormous profits from his crimes. As responsible members of society, you are duty-bound to call a halt to this corruption and see to it that Dr. Himmelstein receives the punishment he fully deserves."

Throughout the proceedings Yosef Aaron retained his composure; it was as if he were unaware of the seriousness of the accusations and the potential consequences. The Rebbe eventually abandoned asking him about the progress of the trial because his responses continued to be far from satisfying. "Don't worry," remained his standard reply. Instead the Rebbe turned to Sidney Levinson, the defense attorney, for an update, and Levinson was considerably less upbeat than Yosef Aaron. As a matter of fact, the lawyer was downright depressed about the developments in court and confided in the Rebbe that Himmelstein's prospects were bleak; the verdict could go either way, and there was no assurance whatsoever of an acquittal.

Two weeks later, as the trial moved into its final stages, Levinson's prognosis turned even more dismal. "I'll fight until the end, Rebbe," he said, "but Ashe has the jury eating out of his hand. I'm saving you for our last character witness, and I am not exaggerating when I tell you that you're also our last hope. Himmelstein's fate depends on your testimony."

The Rebbe knew, of course, that Himmelstein's destiny depended not upon himself but upon the Judge of Judges, but as His earthly emissary the Rebbe recognized the awesome responsibility which had been placed on his shoulders. Although it is halachically forbidden for a Jew to voluntarily subject himself to civil law (as distinct from Jewish Law), the Rebbe knew that in this case his actions were permissible since he would be appearing for the sole purpose of testifying on behalf of an innocent man.

Levinson made it clear that nothing short of the extraordinary would sway the jury in Dr. Himmelstein's favor.

Suddenly an idea occurred to the Rebbe.

With an eye for detail, he carefully dressed for his appearance in court. This, he felt certain, was an element basic to his plan. He donned his *Yom Tov* finery and, from head to toe, was clothed in the attire he knew would make the strongest impression possible on the jury members.

When he arrived at Suffolk Superior Court he noticed what was perhaps a "first" in the annals of regional judicial history: the steps of the courthouse, frequently the venue of protests by Women's Lib activists, student dissidents, the Moral Majority, and anti-Nukers, to name but a few, were on that fateful Tuesday morning graced with scores of Bostoner *chassidim* fervently praying and reciting *Tehillim*.

After some court preliminaries and customary procedure the Rebbe was called upon to testify. Even before this moment all eyes in the courtroom had been focused squarely upon him. The jury appeared to be representative of Boston's demography: two blacks and ten white Catholics, and the Rebbe wondered if anyone present had ever seen a genuine rabbi before, let alone a chassidic Rebbe. Their stares caused him considerable discomfort, but at the same time, a measure of satisfaction: two could play the theatrics game. Clearly, the courtroom was little more than a glorified stage, and the curtain was about to rise.

The Rebbe strode to the stand at a dignified pace befitting a rabbinic figure, and murmured a prayer that the spellbinding aura he had worked to create would hold up.

The court fell silent as the judge, the jury, the defendant, the bailiff, the assistant D.A., the defense attorney, the policemen, and the spectators absorbed every detail of the Rebbe's attire. Their awestuck expressions indicated that his silk brocade caftan was more splendid than any dinner jacket they had ever beheld, his round black hat more unusual than any headgear they'd seen; his flowing beard and *payos* took their breath away. The Rebbe seriously doubted that any Brooks Brothers suit and Princess Mara tie would have impressed them as much or succeeded as well in projecting his credibility as a reliable character witness.

Three steps before the stand the Rebbe nodded respectfully to the judge and asked the honorable magistrate if he might retain his hat during the proceedings. The judge hesitated but a moment before granting his consent. The Rebbe smiled inwardly, knowing that his ploy was having the desired effect.

The Rebbe was asked to state his name and address. This was followed by a question about his position. With a hundred pairs of eyes riveted to him, a hundred pairs of ears straining to hear his every word, and Himmelstein's fate in the balance, the Rebbe knew this was no time for humility. Matter-of-factly he proclaimed that he was a "Grand Rabbi, with thousands of followers and adherents the world over." He was then asked to explain for the jury the office of "Grand Rabbi."

The Rebbe looked directly at the jury members, who by now were all sitting on the edge of their chairs, breathlessly taking in their first encounter with what they clearly considered to be an esteemed personage. An anticipatory silence swept through the courtroom. The Rebbe stroked his beard and responded coolly that the office of Grand Rabbi was analagous to that of a Cardinal. The assembled gasped on cue.

When the Rebbe was sure that information had made its impact, he mentioned that in the thirty years that he had served as Grand Rabbi in New England he had never before entered a courtroom, despite the numerous requests he had received in the past to appear on behalf of coreligionists. The jury foreman exchanged an expressive look with his speechless associates.

By this time it was clear that the gavel had passed to the Rebbe; he held the court's complete, undivided attention. Capitalizing on the opportunity, he stressed that it was not until this day that he had felt obliged to interrupt his rabbinic and communal responsibilities to testify in court; he had done so in this instance because he feared a grave injustice was about to be perpetrated.

The jury was obviously thrilled to be a part of this momentous occasion; the fact that they were gathered to rule upon a major fraud case paled to insignificance. The Rebbe deliberately removed his hat for a moment, revealing his elaborate *yarmulke*, and everyone craned his neck for a glimpse. One woman whispered to her neighbor, "The Cardinal wears only a simple skullcap, but the Grand Rabbi has a whole getup!"

Under Levinson's questioning, the Rebbe extolled Dr. Himmelstein's virtues and stated that he was prepared to stake his reputation on the professor's complete innocence.

Under the circumstances, Yosef Aaron could not have gotten a better character witness, but the Rebbe could not determine if his testimony would mitigate the effects of the preceding weeks in court or the very negative media coverage this trial had received. The prosecution had already presented a mountain of incriminating evidence, and Ashe seemed bent on putting Himmelstein behind bars and winning his promotion.

The assistant D.A. focused his cross-examination on invalidating any points the Rebbe might have scored with his "getup." The Rebbe knew that every word counted now. He had to devise some way to assume the initiative, to counterattack the prosecution. Unwittingly, Ashe provided the opportunity.

Robert Ashe, Esq., D.A.-hopeful and perverter of justice, swaggered the length of the courtroom, aimed a few meaningful glances out the window, and placed his hands on the jury railing. He tilted his head slightly and posed the question which was intended to discount everything the Rebbe had said. "You only know Himmelstein as a member of *and contributor* to your congregation," he began. "He attends religious services with you, but you cannot possibly have any awareness of his activities outside the walls of your synagogue. How, then, can you presume to render an opinion on activities beyond your purview?"

Alarms began sounding in the Rebbe's brain. Ashe had not only put his foot in his mouth but had inadvertently cleared the path to Himmelstein's salvation. The Judge of Judges had delivered the *coup de grace.*

The Rebbe allowed the assembled to see that he was profoundly offended by Ashe's insult. He paused a moment before replying to make sure that everyone present would hang on his every word. As though reading from a script, he declaimed: "On the contrary, sir. As *Grand Rabbi,* I *am* personally aware of *all* of my congregants'

activities within *and beyond* the boundaries of my synagogue. I *am* aware of even the most minute details of their
personal lives." Pause. The Rebbe raised his voice to a
dramatic pitch and extended an accusatory finger toward
the prosecutor. "You, sir, cannot refute this," he intoned,
"for you *yourself* came to interview me regarding Himmelstein's activities outside the synagogue! Not only did you
deem me knowledgeable in *this* regard, but you asked me
for details in regard to Himmelstein's *personal* life! Need I
remind you of your questions concerning the Professor's
life style?"

Completely at a loss for words, Ashe returned to his
desk, flipped through his legal pad, and nervously tapped
his fingers on the desk top. Finally he told the judge that he
had no further questions. He made no other attempts to
impugn the Rebbe's testimony in any way.

THE REBBE did not remain in Boston for the verdict,
although his thoughts were nowhere else but in Suffolk
Superior Court. His *chassidim* later reported that it had
been a very tense moment when the jury foreman, Mr.
Timothy Mulhearny, rose. Even happy-go-lucky Yosef
Aaron Himmelstein had succumbed to the atmosphere of
impending doom, and had blanched nervously.

Mulhearny's announcement of the verdict, "not guilty,"
evoked a roar of victory from the spectators and a chorus
of cheers from the Bostoner *chassidim* who had crowded
into the courtroom.

But the loudest sound heard in the courtroom that day
was the sound of the Celestial Gavel: case dismissed.

26. The Brookline Chassidic Center was purchased in 1960. At the signing were, *standing, left to right*, Samuel S. Schiffman, Edward M. Scherzer, Harry Andler, Jack Rosenberg, Samuel Kulbersh, Edward S. Gerber, Benjamin Green, Sol Gurwitz; *seated, left to right*, Joseph B. Grossman, Samuel Goodman, the Rebbe, and Jack Bardfield (seller).

27. In June 1967, at the height of the Six Day War, a delegation went to Washington to demonstrate on behalf of Israel. Among the delegates were, *left to right*, Linda Gottleib, (unidentifed), Dr. Arnie Hoffman, Avraham Mandel, Andre Garfein, Prof. Louis Shuster of Tufts University, R. Dovid Gottleib (*back, 3rd from right*), and R. Aaron Twersky (*2nd from right*).

28. In 1959, one year before the U.S. Presidency, and conse-
quently the nation, would change forever with the ushering in
of a new era, then-U.S. Senator John F. Kennedy asked to
meet the Rebbe. The Senator's intention was to award honor
and express his esteem for the work the Rebbe had done in
helping immigrants, and to commend the Chassidic Center
for its pivotal role in serving the Jewish community of Boston.

The Rebbe reluctantly agreed to the meeting. Not one to
seek political advantage for *chessed*, the Rebbe was also a bit
apprehensive over what might transpire at this meeting. If, for
example, the senator's wife Jacqueline were to attend, as was
likely, she might expect to shake hands with the Rebbe and
his refusal could create an embarrassing situation. (To the
relief of the Rebbe and his staff, she did not appear.)

Outwardly Jack wore his well-rehearsed smile, but it was
apparent that he too was feeling awkward and unrehearsed in
the company of *chassidim*. Unlike a New York politician who
meets frequently with Rebbes and chassidic leaders, this was
JFK's first encounter with a chassidic court.

In order to break the ice and put the politician at ease, the
Rebbe pointed to some *sefarim* stacked on his desk.
"According to our books and tradition," he said, "one would
never have to resort to the Fifth Amendment to avoid
self-incrimination," alluding to the recent McCarthy hearings
which had rocked the nation. Again and again, witnesses
called before his Senate committee had "claimed the Fifth" to
avoid giving testimony that might impugn their loyalty as
citizens.

"According to Torah law," the Rebbe continued, "even if a
person had indeed admitted participation in an unlawful
activity, his testimony would be invalid." [*Yevamos 25b*].

Senator Kennedy's eyes widened. "How old are these
books?" he asked.

The Rebbe replied that the principle is recorded in the
Talmud, but it dates back to the time the Torah itself was
given, over three millennia ago.

JFK was agog. "Isn't that remarkable," he said with sincere
admiration. "At a time when others coerced innocent people
to admit their guilt by means of torture and inquisition, you
would not even *accept* such testimony!"

29. The Hon. Francis Sargeant, Governor of Massachusetts, signing into law the protection of the rights of Sabbath-observant employees, 1961. Present at this important occasion were State Representative Jon Rotenberg, *2nd from left*; Moses I. Feuerstein, former president of the Orthodox Union, *2nd from right*; and Judah Stone, a noted Boston attorney, *right*.

30. Planning the Brookline *Mikveh* fund-raising campaign, 1964. *Left to right*, Dr. Michael Klein, R. Dovid Rottstein, Dr. Samuel Dershowitz, Prof. Louis Shuster, and Dr. Moshe Singer.

31. The dedication ceremony of the Brookline Chassidic Center, 1961. Among the participants were the Rebbe's brother (then the New York Bostoner Rebbe), R. Moshe Horowitz, *2nd from left*; Samuel Bernstein, father of the famous conductor and composer Leonard Bernstein, *3rd from left*; the Rebbe's brother-in-law, R. Usher Mordechai Rosenbaum, the Strozinitzer Rebbe, *5th from right*; the Rebbe's nephew, R. Avrohom Horowitz (currently the Bostoner Rebbe of New York), *3rd from right*; and the Rebbe's uncle, R. Aaron Yaakov Brandwein, the Torka-Stretener Rebbe, *2nd from right*.

32. Several times a year, the Rebbe hosts a *Shabbaton* at the Chassidic Center for hundreds of college students from the Boston area. Here, the Rebbe recites the *Havdalah* service at the close of the Sabbath.

33. The cafeteria of Brookline High School is converted into a
    Purim festival each year as the Chassidic Center hosts 600-700
    congregants and their children, as well as many college
    students, with a full-course meal, masquerade party and *Purim
    shpiel*. Under the Rebbe's aegis, even a secular school building
    takes on an aura of *kedushah* and becomes a place where
    young people assemble to *daven minchah* and *ma'ariv* and
    partake of the Purim *se'udah*. The "Purim *Rav*" (Dr. Meir
    Wikler) is seen dancing on the table.

34. Selling the *chametz* to Loftus Lewis, a Boston resident originally
    from Jamaica. R. Moshe Perkal of Baltimore served as
    guarantor. This photo was taken by a French sociologist who
    was doing a study of the Bostoner *chassidim* for the Sorbonne.

35. To retain the customs of *Eretz Yisrael*, the Rebbe celebrates
    Lag B'Omer eve in Boston with a simulated (and very modest)
    "bonfire" — in a tin pan! The following morning, the
    traditional *upsharen* is held.

36. Welcoming Russian Jewish immigrants at the Chassidic
    Center. *Right*, Prof. Louis Shuster of Tufts University.

37. When the new addition to the Brookline Chassidic Center was built in 1970, an outstanding Israeli sculptor was commissioned to create a decorative exterior wall that would evoke the image of the Western Wall. His dramatic sculpture, in which a *shofar* and the word שלום — symbolizing the *Ge'ulah* — are hewn on Jerusalem stone, is a source of pride for the entire congregation. Pictured here with the Rebbe are Edward M. Sharzer, *left*, and Harry Andler, *right*, president and vice-president, respectively, of the New England Chassidic Center and active supporters and communal leaders.

38. R.O.F.E.H. Center. The families of patients from all over the world who come to Boston seeking medical treatment are housed in these facilities, in close proximity to the Chassidic Center. All their needs — physical and spiritual — are seen to by the Bostoner Rebbe and his *chassidim*.

38

39. Award ceremony at Deaconess Hospital, 1978. *Left to right,* C. Stephen Bressler, acting commissioner, Brookline Human Relations Commission and president, Congregation Beth Pinchas, Brookline; Lawrence MacLure, president, New England Deaconess Hospital; Dr. Wilford Neptune, Award recipient, Overholt Thoracic Clinic, New England Deaconess Hospital; the Rebbe presenting the award; Dr. Samuel Hellman, Award recipient, chairman, Department of Radiation Therapy, Harvard Medical Schools Joint Center; William Ginsburg, Director of Development, Beth Israel Hospital; Laibel Marshall, coordinator, Project R.O.F.E.H.; the Rebbetzin.

40. At the R.O.F.E.H. Dinner, 1987. *Seated, left to right*: R.W. Striar, Man of the Year; the Rebbe; Dr. William Silen, R.O.F.E.H. award recipient; Eugene Buckwald, Director of Brigham and Women's and Beth Israel Hospitals, Professor of Medicine at Harvard University. *Standing, left to right*: the Rebbe's son, Reb Naftali; Daniel Striar; Samuel Schiffman; Martin Hoffman; Dr. Brian Blackburn, Massachusetts Medical Examiner; Justin Wyner, Dinner chairman; Mr. Avraham Avnon, Israeli Consul General; Dr. Fred Mandal, Chief of Pediatrics, Boston Children's Hospital; Dr. Izy Perle.

41. The Rebbe with Dr. Kurt Isselbacher, Chief of the Gastrointestinal Unit and Director of the Cancer Center, Massachusetts General Hospital.

42. The Rebbe with Dr. Robert Mayer, *center*, Director of Medical Services, and Dr. Emil Frei III, Director of the world-famous Dana-Farber Cancer Institute.

43. Dr. Alexander Nades, Chief of Cardiology at Boston Children's Hospital, receives a R.O.F.E.H. citation. *Left to right*, Judge Sumner Kaplan, R.O.F.E.H. Awards Dinner chairman; the Rebbe; Dr. Nades; Dr. Fred Mandal, Chief of Pediatrics at Boston Children's Hospital.

44. The Rebbe with Dr. Bernard Lown, a noted cardiologist and Nobel Prize Laureate.

45. In one of the Rebbe's first endeavors leading to *aliyah* to *Eretz Yisrael*, he coordinated the delivery of several Torah scrolls donated by a Bostoner *chassid* to the Mercaz Harav Yeshiva, 1964. Holding the *sefer Torah* is the noted *tzaddik* of Jerusalem, Zushia Brandwein.

46. *Hoshanah Rabbah*, 1975. The Rebbe's second son, R. Mayer, *left*, later became *Rav* of Givat Pinchas in Har Nof. His youngest son, R. Naftali, *right*, is presently Rav of the Beth Pinchos Chassidic Center in Brookline.

47. At the *Kenessiah Gedolah* of Agudath Israel in Jerusalem, 1981.
Left to right, R. Shneur Kotler; R. Shmuel Weinberg, *standing*;
the Rebbe; the Gerer Rebbe; R. Shach, *Rosh Yeshiva* of
Ponovezh; R. Avrohom Yosef Lazerson, Deputy Mayor of
Jerusalem; R. S. Grossbard, Director of *Chinnuch Atzmai*; R.
Yaakov Ruderman; R. Yaakov Kamenetsky.

48. R. Shneur Kotler at the Chassidic Center on behalf of the
Lakewood Yeshiva. *Left to right*, R. Mordechai Savitsky; R.
Shneur Kotler; R. Josef B. Soloveitchik; R. Leibel Cywiak,
standing; the Rebbe; R. Hirsh Tannenbaum of Chelsea; R.
Henry Landes of Revere.

49. The Rebbe visits the grave of his ancestor, R. Pinchas
Horowitz, the "Hafla"ah," *zt"l*, Frankfurt-am-Main, 1987.

A Flight from Kennedy

Wednesday morning in the Rebbe's study. Outside, a hot July day is beginning, the Green Line streetcar is busy collecting commuters into parking-starved downtown Boston, and Baskin Robbins is opening its doors for what promises to be a busy day. Inside, Leibel Wattstein is conscientiously receiving the Rebbe's instructions about getting a *chessed* project underway, and downstairs a *minyan* for late risers is in full swing.

Just as the Rebbe reached a critical point in his directives to Leibel, the phone rang. It was a woman who identified herself as Mrs. Katz from Baltimore. The Rebbe had never met her before, but it was very clear from her agitated tone that she needed his help immediately. It was hard to grasp everything she said as the connection was poor, a problem exacerbated by her hysterical state.

The woman explained that she had been visiting her nine-year-old son, Barry, in a summer camp in Maine when he was hit by a car. Barry was rushed to the local hospital, a facility ill-equipped to deal properly with the emergency, and the boy's condition was grave. If he pulled through, she said, he would need immediate orthopedic surgery to prevent his being crippled for life, and the closest and most reliable venue for such an operation was Massachusetts General Hospital, in Boston.

According to Mrs. Katz, Barry could not be transferred by ambulance because of the poor condition of the roads. Furthermore, the eight-hour trip was too long a period for him to be without intensive care. The hospital had informed her that the only way to transfer the patient was via private plane, which could leave from a small airfield nearby.

This incident occurred more than a quarter of a century ago, before the introduction of aerial ambulance services. Had it happened more recently, the problem could have been solved in a straightforward fashion, but in 1962 it required a bit of legerdemain. The Rebbe wondered if he possessed the dexterity necessary to pull an airplane out of his hat.

The Rebbe told Mrs. Katz that although he was not personally acquainted with an owner of a private plane, he would make every effort to get hold of one. He took down all of the pertinent details and got right to work.

Leibel began to look up the phone numbers of anyone and everyone the Rebbe could think of who might possibly be a candidate, and dialed one after another in rapid succession. But apparently aviation was not a particularly popular pastime among the Rebbe's circle of associates, and he had no success.

Meanwhile the minutes were ticking away, and the

Rebbe's involvement in emergencies such as these had taught him that time was always of the essence. From what Mrs. Katz had said he knew that a few hours could mean the difference between her son's being able to walk normally again and being permanently confined to a wheelchair, maybe even between life and death.

This sense of urgency, however, was in no way helping his radar track an airplane, until an outrageous idea occurred to him. Since private planes were not very much in vogue, he should not have been looking to the private sector for assistance; instead of contacting megabucks, he concluded, he should be contacting mega*connections*.

There was one individual who qualified in that regard, and although the Rebbe actually knew him personally, he hesitated to presume on their acquaintance. His inner voice pitched a stiff battle against his reason, encouraging him to make the move. "Go to the top!" it argued. "He came to *you* when he needed *your* help."

There was no denying that. The Rebbe asked Leibel to find the number and instantly his faithful assistant stood at attention, chin thrust forward, hands riveted to his sides. "The number, Leibel," the Rebbe urged, snapping his fingers to break the spell, but Leibel was firmly entranced, his eyes fixed straight ahead at nothing.

"Leibel, LEIBEL!" the Rebbe called loudly, and life began to stir within. Starry-eyed and nearly swooning, Leibel asked if the Rebbe had meant the telephone number of *the* White House, the White House in which the *President*, chief of the executive branch, JFK *himself*, lived.

If he hadn't been dealing with a medical emergency the Rebbe might have been tempted to respond with one of several witty remarks that came to mind, but this was no time for jest. Instead he simply replied in the affirmative and gestured for Leibel to get on with it.

The Rebbe's inner voice had accurately reminded him that John Fitzgerald Kennedy had indeed approached him on several occasions seeking his support for local and national elections. Could the Rebbe dare to ask the President of the United States to return the favor? On the other hand, could he not? After all, the Rebbe was engaged in a lifesaving activity, and he was presenting the President with a golden opportunity to lend a hand, the sort of thing JFK had built his reputation on. The worst Jack could do was turn the Rebbe down. Would he refuse a request from a friend and neighbor? the Rebbe wondered. That was how *he'd* phrased *his* request for the Rebbe's support. Of course, he realized that a presidential hopeful born in Brookline a mere two blocks away from the Chassidic Center was somewhat more accessible than the leader of the western world, but that didn't daunt the Rebbe. He dialed the long-distance operator and gave her the number Leibel had so patriotically provided.

"White House, good morning," a female voice responded to a listing they had gotten from the Washington, D.C. directory. The Rebbe was astonished to have gotten through with such ease, not realizing at first that he was nowhere *near* the Oval Office; he was speaking to a switchboard operator whose job it was to impress elementary school children who called up Washington for the thrill of it.

Casting aside his inhibitions, the Rebbe asked if the President was in, and identified himself as the President's good friend, Grand Rabbi Levi Horowitz, from Boston.

"One moment, please," she said, and transferred the call to a secretary. He repeated his introduction and the secretary transferred him to her superior. He went through the very same procedure four more times, each time emphasizing the "good friend" and "Boston," until at last he was transferred to the President's personal administrative assistant's aide.

Once again the Rebbe introduced himself in what was by now a polished routine, and the aide said, "Let me connect you with the administrative offices." No doubt if Nikita Khrushchev had had to go through all of this to speak to the President, *his* call would have been collect!

The Rebbe reached the assistant to the director of the administrative office and recited his intro once more. He begged to speak to the President right away, as he was calling regarding an issue of the utmost urgency, a matter of life and death.

The assistant detected the sincerity of the caller's request and yet again the Rebbe found himself "on hold." By this time he figured he must be in the President's own living room. At least. Instead, he ended up speaking to another link in the chain of command, and he continued to climb higher and higher, getting the maximum mileage from his tax dollars. After nine transfers, five connections and three "one moment, please"s the Rebbe was convinced it was sheer luck that Jacqueline didn't pick up the receiver herself!

The final person he reached was obviously as high as one could get with a conventionally wired phone. This fellow was neither an aide, a director, nor an executive; he was the President's personal assistant, a fellow the Rebbe had actually been privileged to meet once or twice. He recognized the Rebbe's name instantly and even remembered that he was from Brookline. The President's P.A. asked the Rebbe very detailed questions and this time the Rebbe was confident his message would make its way directly to JFK.

Apologetically, the P.A. informed the Rebbe that Jack was unavailable. "He must be airborne by now," he said. "He's en route to the Compound." The Rebbe correctly understood that to mean the Kennedy family estate in Hyannis Port, Massachusetts.

"Is there any way that I can reach him?" the Rebbe asked.

The P.A. assured him that his message would be relayed as soon as possible. The Rebbe dictated the phone number of his "private line," praying that if the President did in fact return his call, the Chassidic Center's one and only phone would not be engaged at that precise moment by one of the numerous residents.

Precious time had been lost over this runaround, and with Barry Katz's life dangling by a very tenuous thread, the Rebbe did not wish to rely exclusively on the Chief Executive's chief executive. He applied his crisis-honed mind to the problem and a more local and, admittedly, more logical solution came to him.

Rather than throw poor Leibel into shell shock a second time, the Rebbe looked up this phone number himself. Getting through to a secretary competent to take a message was less complicated in Senator Ted Kennedy's Boston office than in his big brother's, and one of the first individuals the Rebbe spoke to informed him that the Senator was in the capital. She gave the Rebbe the number of his direct line.

Mr. Sanford Dunlap answered the phone, recognized the Rebbe's name, and was very accommodating. He told the Rebbe that the Senator had just left with Jack for Hyannis Port, but asked how he could help.

The Rebbe was about to tell him that he needed the Senator's intervention for a medical emergency, but realizing that the Senator must receive hundreds of appeals for humanitarian causes, the Rebbe felt he should try a different approach. He knew that unless he had an unusual angle, or could haul out a mighty favor that had yet to be reciprocated, his request stood little chance of earning immediate attention.

The seeds of an idea quickly germinated in his head. Nine months earlier the Senator had been running for office in a tightly contested race. His opponent, Edward McCormick, seemed to have the edge, and Kennedy was reaching out to whomever he could for support and endorsement.

Naturally, as representative of a sizeable portion of the constituency, the Rebbe held a prominent place on Ted's list. He received repeated phone calls from Kennedy's campaign manager complaining that Blue Hill Avenue in Dorchester, a predominantly Jewish area better known as "Jew Hill" Avenue, was liberally plastered with McCormick posters. Aware of the Rebbe's policy of neutrality during political races, the campaign manager asked if Ted could just "be received" in the Chassidic Center, to demonstrate the community's evenhandedness. Such a gesture, he figured, would provide valuable publicity in the Blue Hill Avenue area for the Senate hopeful.

Despite his misgivings, the Rebbe didn't see how he could refuse the request. Thus one week later a reception was held at the Chassidic Center, an event which was later intepreted by political analysts as a turning point in the campaign, resulting in a Kennedy victory. The rookie Senator was very grateful to the Rebbe at the time, and asked him, in not so many words, why he had agreed to do the favor.

The Rebbe seized the opportunity to sanctify the Almighty's name by explaining to the Catholic politician the Jewish concept of performing a *mitzvah*. When one is in a position to help, the Rebbe said, it is incumbent upon him to do so. Indeed whenever confronted with a *mitzvah* situation, one has a sacred obligation to do his utmost. Little did the Rebbe know then that his brief excursus would later reap substantial dividends.

Banking on Kennedy's memory, the Rebbe told Sanford Dunlap that he needed the Senator's help to perform a *mitzvah*.

"Pardon me, a what?" Dunlap asked.

"A *mitzvah*," the Rebbe repeated.

"Would you spell that, please?"

"M-I-T-Z-V-A-H."

"I, er...don't know if the Senator is familiar with the term," Sanford stammered. "Could you elaborate?"

"Certainly," the Rebbe said, and related the entire Katz saga, underscoring the urgency of the matter.

Dunlap asked the Rebbe for specific details: time, place, phone numbers, which he readily supplied. Thanking the

Senator's aide for his interest, the Rebbe hung up the phone.

SOMEWHERE in rural Maine a Jewish boy's life was on the line. The Rebbe knew that he had done all that he could to secure transportation to a superb medical facility, yet he was suffering an acute anxiety attack. He was accustomed to dealing with medical emergencies; he does so daily. Invariably, once he implements a course of action, his mind is at ease, knowing that he has done what the Almighty has entrusted him to do. But in this case, he had no solace. The problem was far from resolved, the outcome of his efforts uncertain, and his apprehension was keen.

The Rebbe sat at his desk agonizingly contemplating other courses he might follow. He had left messages with both Jack and Ted; it would appear utterly foolish to call again. Time passed inexorably, and the Rebbe feared for the life of the injured child.

It wasn't until five-thirty in the afternoon that he received a progress report, and his adrenaline surged. Mrs. Katz was on the line, thanking the Rebbe profusely for having arranged the air transport. The Rebbe didn't let on that this was the first he'd heard about it.

What he was able to piece together from her understandably disjointed report was that early in the afternoon she'd gotten a call from the airport in Bangor, Maine informing her that a Northeast Airlines jet was about to arrive at the local airstrip to take her son to Boston.

The Rebbe heaved a great sigh of relief — but at the same time, cringed with chagrin. A commercial jet had been sent on a mission of mercy! He had assumed that if anything, a Coast Guard propeller plane would be dispatched; a commercial aircraft meant commercial costs, and the Rebbe had never bargained for this.

As it happened both his relief and his distress were premature: the clincher was yet to come. As though relating a superfluous detail, Mrs. Katz informed the Rebbe that her son would not be flying to Boston at present because the hospital would not release him until 10:00 the following morning.

"Tomorrow?!" the Rebbe exclaimed, unable to keep the note of apprehension from his voice.

"I hope so," Mrs. Katz responded. "You see my son's abdominal aorta ruptured in the accident — they only discovered the internal bleeding after I had spoken to you. He has just undergone surgery to repair the blood vessel and the doctor says that he must stabilize overnight before he can travel."

The Rebbe knew the doctor was right, but his mind was clouded with visions of dollar bills sprouting wings and mountains of unpaid debts to politicians. "How will you get to Mass. General?" he asked at last.

"Don't worry, Rebbe," Barry's mother assured him. "Everything is arranged. I had a talk with that nice pilot and he said he'd come back tomorrow…"

The Rebbe swallowed hard as the price of this favor escalated exponentially. Mrs. Katz droned on.

"…He's going to spend the night in a local hotel, and I'm to ring him as soon as we're ready to fly. How can I ever thank you for taking care of everything!"

The Rebbe wished he could have told her, but it would have been cruel to place an additional burden on her by revealing the astronomical expense of the transportation. Although he knew little about the cost of air travel, he figured the liability totalled at least five digits, not taking into account overtime for the pilot, his hotel bill, and airport charges. All he could do was wish Barry a heartfelt *refuah shelemah.*

The fear that the bill for services rendered would be mailed to his address — or Mrs. Katz's, for that matter! — overwhelmed him. Every time he thought about it, a new expense came to mind and the cost kept skyrocketing. As he was tallying the figures for the umpteenth time, the phone rang again and the Rebbe answered it with great trepidation. It was Sanford Dunlap in Washington.

Sanford was calling to say that a plane had been dispatched earlier in the day to pick up the boy and bring him to Boston for the emergency operation. He conveyed Ted's personal regards and told the Rebbe that the President was also being kept abreast of developments. Proudly, he detailed how Ted himself had arranged for the plane from Northeast. "The Senator wants to know if his help is needed at Mass. General — the family does have a bit of pull there, you know."

"Everything has been taken care of with the hospital," the Rebbe replied, more curtly than he'd intended. He didn't have the heart — or the nerve — to inform Dunlap that the plane wouldn't be leaving until the following day. He thanked Sanford for bringing him up to date and asked the aide to communicate his profound gratitude to both the President and the Senator.

SLEEP ALLUDED the Rebbe that night. He paced the floor wondering how to break the news to the Senator. He had no doubt that this was the last favor he would ever be able to request from him. Even more perturbing was the onerous debt for which the Rebbe knew *he* was ultimately responsible. The figures he had calculated earlier echoed harrowingly in his brain, compounding an already excruciating headache.

In the wee hours of the morning, the Rebbe devised a way to mitigate the damages, or in plain English, to get a discount. He would suggest that since Barry would be landing in Boston around noon the next day, Ted might want to be on hand to greet him. He would tell Dunlap that this would be a wonderful opportunity for the Senator to demonstrate his unflinching devotion to humanitarianism. The press would be sure to take notice of this magnanimous deed, and Teddy wouldn't want to look like a piker — he'd surely offer to pick up the tab, or some part thereof. The plan was outrageously simple, but the Rebbe was confident it would work.

At nine o'clock on the dot he called up Senator Kennedy's office, and the very affable Mr. Dunlap came on the line. "I don't know how to even *begin* to thank you, the Senator, and all of your dedicated staff," the Rebbe began. "Each and every one of you is a paragon of human kindness, people who know the true meaning of brotherhood."

"I'm glad we could be of service, Rabbi."

The Rebbe stalled for time, conjuring up any other compliment he could think of even remotely related to the subject at hand, until finally he blurted out, "I don't know how to break it to you and the Senator, especially after all that you have done, but there was a slight hitch in the emergency transfer…Eh, due to medical complications the young man could not be released from the hospital until this morning. The pilot…"

"Yes, yes," Dunlap interrupted, "we know all about it, Rabbi. All of the arrangements have been made."

"I…I," the Rebbe hesitated, trying to phrase his ingenious suggestion effectively, but in the face of the Kennedys' gracious and unstinting cooperation, the idea suddenly seemed like a cheap ploy.

"I will be eternally grateful for the Senator's intercession on behalf of this child," he told Sanford. "I sincerely hope it wasn't a major inconvenience for him." There was no point in even bringing up his publicity stunt idea; the Rebbe knew he'd have to bear the consequences of his actions like a man.

"I'll be sure to convey your gratitude, Rabbi."

The Rebbe was about to hang up when Sanford remembered something. "I almost forgot," he said. "The Senator asked me to give you an important message. He asked me to tell you — wait just a minute while I get it. I have it written down somewhere…" The sound of papers being shuffled — *bills* being shuffled — came across the line.

"Yes, here it is," Dunlap said at last and the Rebbe held his breath, waiting for the ax to fall. "Ted asked me to tell you, and I hope I say this right: 'One good *mitzvah* deserves another.'"

The End
of the Road

When the Rebbe first met Cindy Fried she was a vivacious Boston University coed just starting out on the road to Torah living. Always modestly attired, Cindy impressed everyone as a sensitive and intelligent person, serious about her studies, both secular and religious. She would drop by the Chassidic Center from time to time to participate in one of the many activities for young adults, and often stop in to visit with the Rebbetzin.

There was a remark that was popular among collegiates on campus in the seventies: "Don't let college interfere with your college life," a reflection of the general attitude of flippancy that pervaded the student body with regard to their studies; their social life, on the other hand, they pursued with great zest. Cindy didn't let college interfere with her Judaism, and her zest to perform *mitzvos* was exhilarating — at times, one might say, exhausting.

By the time Cindy was a sophomore it was not unusual for her to arrive late at night at the Rebbe's house to help the Rebbetzin out with some household chore or other. This, needless to say, was after an evening of babysitting or running errands for the overburdened mothers in the community. *Chessed* was her primary extracurricular activity.

Whenever Cindy would appear, be it late at night or early in the morning, her face was always graced with a smile, a friendly greeting on her lips. Her exuberance and élan, the Rebbe was told by numerous students from Boston University and other schools in the area, was not restricted to the Chassidic Center. She had developed a cadre of dedicated followers whom she helped gather under the wings of Judaism.

The voice on the phone Sunday evening, however, was not the Cindy the Rebbe knew. Her words were punctuated by mournful sobbing, such that he was unable to understand what she was saying. Finally, she managed to articulate, "Rebbe, I'm in trouble..."

The Rebbe's heart skipped a beat. Those buzz words never fail to move him, four little words that are always the harbinger of very ominous tidings.

Cindy lapsed into a fit of crying and could say no more. The Rebbe tried to imagine what her problem might be. She was engaged to a boy whom she had met at the Chassidic Center and all agreed that theirs was a perfect match. Both were newly religious and thoroughly committed to their Judaism and to each other. The wedding, at which the Rebbe was to officiate, was scheduled for two weeks hence. Surely nothing could have gone wrong with that *shidduch.*

The Rebbe's attempts to ascertain the nature of Cindy's problem were in no way helped by the crying coming over the line. "I don't know what to do," she said at last, her voice laced with sorrow. "I'm supposed to get married at the end of the month, and I just learned that I'm...that I'm a...*mamzer!*"*

The Rebbe flinched as though he'd suffered a physical blow. Over the past three years he and the Rebbetzin had had the pleasure, indeed the honor, of watching Cindy flower into the exceptional *bas Torah* she was. She had become a *bas bayis* in their home, and the Chassidic Center benefited immeasurably from her presence. She'd had every hope of building a genuine *bayis ne'eman b'Yisrael*, a home imbued with Torah values and filled with the joys of Jewish living, and now it appeared those hopes were dashed.

"Cindy," the Rebbe said gently, "I don't know why you suspect that you might not be a legitimate *bas Yisrael*, but *mamzerus* is a somewhat esoteric, and very technical halachic term, and it is often misinterpreted. Why don't you come over and we'll talk about it?"

While the Rebbe waited for her to arrive at the Chassidic Center, he reviewed the stipulations of *mamzerus* in his mind. One possibility was that one of Cindy's parents was a *mamzer* — the product of a forbidden union, such as that of a son and his mother, a father and his daughter, a brother and his sister, etc. — which would render her one as well.

Another possibility was that Cindy's parents' marriage constituted a forbidden union. These instances of *mamzerus* are rare, but when dealing with people who are unaware of or unconcerned with *Halachah*, anything is

* An illegitimate child, forbidden by Jewish law to marry a legitimate Jew.

possible, even though society as a whole frowns upon such unions...It was more likely, though, the Rebbe thought, that Cindy's mother had not been properly divorced from her former husband before marrying Cindy's father. Such an instance of *mamzerus*, tragically commonplace these days, results when a kosher *get* has not been delivered.

The frequency of such cases, coupled with Cindy's tearful words, "...I just learned...", made the Rebbe conclude that her prospects were bleak. The sight of the grief-stricken young woman at the door augmented his concern.

The Rebbetzin escorted Cindy into the study and placed a box of Kleenex at her side. Cindy made quick work of the tissues even before she commenced her tale of woe; her sobbing plunged them all into a state of deep despair. The saga was but four hours old, yet its ramifications would affect, and conceivably ruin, a lifetime.

Earlier that afternoon at her university, a noted Torah scholar had lectured on the sanctity of marriage. In the course of his talk he explained that the term *mamzer* does *not* necessarily apply to a child born out of wedlock (a common misconception), but to one born of a woman who has remarried without receiving a *get* from her previous husband.

"Even before the lecture was over," Cindy related, "I rushed out to call home. I confronted my mother and insisted that she tell me if her first husband had given her a *get*. As you know, Rebbe, my mother is not at all religious, and I doubted she'd ever bothered about a *get*. She wouldn't answer my question, and when I pressed her, she became very flustered. 'Why do you want to know?' she asked. 'Because it affects me in the most serious way,' I said. I begged her to be honest with me because my future depended upon her answer."

"And how did she react to that?" the Rebbe asked.

"With a tirade against religious observance." Cindy frowned at the memory of her mother's words. "She's been against my embracing Judaism from the outset. 'You chose this absurd way of life,' she scolded, 'this cult of yours. Now your belief will bury you!' Then she said, 'This is the end of the road, kid,' and broke the connection.

"Rebbe," Cindy whispered, dissolving once again in tears, "I...I think she's right. It *is* the end of the road for me."

Sad to say, although the Rebbe has had to deal with terrible, devastating situations like this in the past, experience didn't make it any easier. The plight of this sweet young girl, a *neshamaleh* who had practically grown up in his home, was like a knife in his heart. The Rebbetzin was dabbing at her eyes and the Rebbe too was on the verge of tears.

He entreated the *Ribbono shel Olam* to spare Cindy from the tragic fate of being a *mamzer*. He prayed for an *eitzah*, anything that might confirm her legitimacy. One idea, a solitary hope, crept into his mind and the Rebbe cautiously pursued it.

"Cindy," he said, "tell me about your childhood, about your relationship with your parents."

"Wh-what?"

"Just tell me how things were with you and your parents when you were a child," he repeated. "Did you have a happy childhood?"

"My parents were divorced when I was six years old,"

she repled softly. "This was Mom's second divorce. Up until their separation, I guess you could say I had a happy childhood."

"But you do remember your father, don't you?"

"Oh, yes. I loved my father and we were very close. He always took me on outings to the zoo and to an amusement park in the area. He read me a story practically every night at bedtime, and he would play catch with me on weekends.

"I knew there were problems between him and Mom. Even though I was very young I can still remember their bitter arguments...Rebbe, I realize that you're only asking me these questions to calm me down and make me think about happier times. But I'm not a six-year-old any more; I'm a young woman and my life has been ruined. I love David and now I can never marry..."

"Let's not be hasty, Cindy," the Rebbe interrupted. "I am asking you these questions because they are relevant. A *mamzer* is only a *mamzer* if it is certain that the criteria for *mamzerus* have been met, and I'm not yet convinced they have. A harangue or two from your mother is really not sufficient grounds for determining your status. The situation certainly warrants a little more serious investigation, wouldn't you say?"

Cindy nodded her reluctant agreement and the Rebbe resumed his line of questioning, hoping to uncover something which might invalidate her being a *mamzer*. He had to keep digging until he was positive that there was nothing, nothing at all, left to uncover. Considering the attitude of Cindy's mother, the Rebbe thought it might prove more productive if he were to speak to Cindy's father, Mr. George Fried, instead.

"Are you still in contact with your father?" he asked.

"No, Rebbe. No one knows where he is; he has simply vanished. Last year I wanted to send him a birthday card so I called my grandparents, but even they —"

"Grandparents?" the Rebbe cried excitedly. "Your paternal grandparents? They're alive? Where do they live?"

"In Dallas," Cindy replied, startled by the Rebbe's keen interest in this detail.

He grabbed the phone as Cindy fished in her purse for her pocket phone directory. She read the Texas number to him and he quickly punched in the digits. After several rings, an elderly Mr. Fried answered, and the Rebbe identified himself, explaining that he was calling about a very important matter.

Cindy's grandfather responded to all of the Rebbe's questions but made no significant contribution. He confirmed everything his granddaughter had already reported, and had no additional information to volunteer. Disheartened, the Rebbe was about to hang up when a different angle occurred to him.

"Did your son have a *bar mitzvah*?" he asked.

Instead of replying right away with a simple yes or no, Mr. Fried covered the mouthpiece and a muffled conference between him and, presumably, his wife, took place. The Rebbe wondered why they needed to consult before answering such a straightforward question. Perhaps, he thought, they were ashamed that they had not done the most obvious and basic thing for their son.

Finally the grandmother got on the line and told the Rebbe that George had been "confirmed" at the local temple when he was thirteen. She passed the phone back to her husband.

Something indefinable prompted the Rebbe to ask the next question: "Was that the same temple where he had his *bris*, that is, his circumcision?" he inquired. Silence followed, then some awkward hemming and hawing. The Rebbe asked Cindy if she would step out of the study so that he might continue the conversation in private.

There was something definitely awry. Without waiting for their reply, the Rebbe asked the Frieds where George had been born. Again a direct response was not forthcoming. It didn't require any piercing analysis or brilliant deduction to conclude that George Fried was a mystery baby.

The Rebbe asked Cindy's grandfather if there was an extension phone in the house. There was. He requested that Mrs. Fried get on the extension as he had a crucial question to ask and he wanted them both to hear it.

Before posing his query the Rebbe explained that while under normal circumstances he would never pry into someone's personal life, these were not normal circumstances. "Cindy's future is at stake," the Rebbe declared and paused for the words to sink in. Only when he was certain that they grasped the gravity of the situation did he proceed to detail his relationship with their granddaughter.

"I am a rabbi," he said, "a chassidic rebbe, in fact, if that means anything to you. Will you accept my word that what you tell me I will never reveal to a living soul?"

"Yes, Rabbi," they said apprehensively.

In a somber voice the Rebbe asked them if in fact their son was adopted.

They hesitated for a while and the Rebbe implored them to be frank with him. After what seemed an eternity, Mrs. Fried confessed that they had adopted their son at the age of 15 months. No one, she said, including George himself, was aware of this. She told the Rebbe that although they had wanted to adopt a Jewish baby, they had been unable to get one and had to accept a child whose natural mother was Gentile.* The Frieds had never formally converted him to Judaism.

"*Baruch Hashem*," the Rebbe sighed, and resumed breathing. He could not remember ever being so happy to learn that a Jew was not a Jew. Since George Fried was not Jewish, Cindy was technically not a *mamzer*. *Mamzerus* applies only to the offspring of a forbidden union between *Jews*. Cindy could marry her David.

The Rebbe thanked the Frieds profusely for the information and told them that he was looking forward to meeting them at Cindy's wedding. He hung up the phone and almost danced out of his office to relate the wonderful news.

He found their *bas bayis* sitting in the kitchen with the Rebbetzin, lamenting her fate in a barely audible voice. The Rebbetzin looked at her husband peculiarly, most likely due to the fact that he was crying — crying with joy. He was so overcome that for a moment he could not speak.

"My dear *kallah*," the Rebbe announced, finding his voice at last, "this is not the end of the road at all. It is only the beginning."

---

* The Rebbe later received independent confirmation of this.

Weather or Not

The big day was approaching, and the storm for which Boston had been bracing itself arrived on schedule with all its fury: gale-force winds, driving rain bursting the floodgates of the heavens, and cloud cover so heavy that day seemed like night. Normally, inclement weather did not bother the Rebbe, but it was Monday, only two days away from Wednesday, and Wednesday was to be a very important day.

Wednesday's importance, it should be noted, was contingent upon clear skies. The Talmud teaches that a wise man prepares for the future, and the Rebbe had every intention of earning that honorific. There had been plenty of time to prepare in this case, since it was an occasion for which advance notice had been given twenty-eight years earlier! Wednesday was to be the day of *Birkas Ha-chammah*.

Birkas Ha-chammah, the blessing over the sun, is a benediction made only once every twenty-eight years, when the sun returns to the precise position where God placed it on the day of its creation. But this once-in-three-decades blessing can only be recited if the object of the blessing is revealed in all its glory.

For months the Rebbe had anticipated this special milestone and contemplated what he could do to ensure that the weather would not frustrate his plans for celebrating the occasion. The opportunity was such a rare one — it would be a pity to have to miss it because of one intransigent thunderhead. New England weather conditions are unpredictable in April, and precipitation of one sort or another is not at all uncommon then.

The Rebbe's father, the first Bostoner Rebbe, of blessed memory, had faced a similar dilemma twenty-eight years before. Weeks in advance, he had "followed the sun," and his heart, to the Holy Land, thereby relieving himself of the climatic anxiety that the Rebbe was now suffering. Simultaneously, he had assured himself of a spiritually uplifting environment and plenty of pious company.

The Rebbe likewise entertained thoughts of traveling to *Eretz Yisrael*, but that would have entailed abandoning his flock for the Passover season. Unlike his father, however, the Rebbe had the advantage of living in the age of aviation, and if necessary could escape a locally overcast sky with relative ease.

With less than two days to go before the time of the blessing, and the lowering skies an ominous mass of cumulonimbus, the Rebbe began to make his contingency plan. Step one was to determine the forecast for Wednesday — there was no point in booking a flight out of the area if the weather was going to clear in time — and to this end, he had Leibel telephone a Boston radio station.

"Hello? I'm calling for Grand Rabbi Levi Horowitz," Wattstein announced importantly. "Is the weatherman there?"

The switchboard operator put him through to Cal Lacy, but upon hearing the voice of a genuine media celebrity, poor Leibel went into catatonic shock.

Gingerly the Rebbe extracted the receiver from his assistant's frozen grip and placed it against his ear. "Talk fast," a disembodied voice was saying, "I gotta get back into the sound room in forty seconds."

"Are you the weatherman?" the Rebbe asked.

"Look, mister," Lacy replied irritably, "if you got complaints about the weather..."

"No, no," the Rebbe protested, "I'm not calling to complain. I'd just like to ask about the long-range forecast."

"Sorry, mister," Lacy said, speaking rapidly, "I'm not the forecaster. I just read the copy. You want the forecast, call the weather bureau."

The Rebbe roused Leibel from his stupor and directed him to proceed with his mission. Wattstein dialed the weather bureau. After posing the $64-question, he nodded mutely into the phone, raised his eyebrows expressively, muttered several "Mm-hmm"s and hung up. Then he headed for the front door.

"Er, Leibel," the Rebbe called after him, "what did they say?"

"They said, 'If you want to know the weather,'" he quoted faithfully, "'go outside. If you get wet, it's raining; if you start sweating, it's a sunny day.' So I'm going out to check."

The Rebbe asked him to dial again, this time taking care

to get the right number, and Leibel cheerfully complied. "I wasn't really anxious to go out in the storm, Rebbe," he said.

"I wouldn't think so," the Rebbe commented drily. "See if you can get the director of the bureau on the line — we'll go straight to the top."

In his typically conscientious fashion, Leibel persevered until he'd gotten through to the Chief Meteorologist of New England. He passed the phone to the Rebbe. "If this guy doesn't know the weather, Rebbe, *nobody* does."

"Dr. Marvin Woltersdorf here," the oddly high-pitched voice answered. "How can I help you?"

The Rebbe told him simply that he wanted to know the week's forecast, unaware that for a specialist like Dr. Woltersdorf, nothing was "simple." The meteorologist treated him to a host of barometric pressure readings, recited some weatherese mumbo jumbo about high isobars over the West Indies and other related, or for all the Rebbe knew, unrelated data, followed by a filibuster regarding the overall climate variations anticipated in every region of the continental United States.

"A high pressure ridge extending 20,000 feet above sea level," he squeaked, "will send warm, dry air into the Texas panhandle, sweeping across the western Plains. Light winds and clear skies associated with high pressure at the Gulf Coast will allow a haze to form early in the morning from the lower Texas Coast into the Ohio River Valley. But," he hastily added, "the fog will quickly dissipate.

"A relatively weak, low-pressure system will traverse the Great Lakes," he went on with alacrity, "producing some cirrostratus and mammatocumulus cloud formations and isolated pockets of precipitation. Light snow flurries may graze northern New York State. The circulation about a high pressure area off Maine will bring cool sea air to southern New England, keeping coastal areas 5 to 10 degrees cooler than the interior."

"Wait!" the Rebbe interjected, trying to get Woltersdorf to focus on the Boston area, but the Chief Meteorologist of New England seemed duty-bound to provide him with a complete picture.

"...Warmer air will return to Florida after several days of unseasonable cold. Squalls associated with an offshore disturbance will move farther east over the Atlantic. A disorganized area of showers will extend from the Northern Rockies to the Pacific. A jet stream rotating around an intense storm in the Gulf of Alaska will produce periods of steady rainfall from northern California to Idaho, but there will also be extensive intervals with no rain and partly cloudy skies. Arctic air over much of Canada will slide south behind a cold front. High pressure will push the cold air into the northern plains and Great Lakes states, returning temperatures to seasonable levels."

There was a brief hiatus in the good doctor's recitation, but apparently he was merely pausing to catch his breath.

"...It should be borne in mind that a warm front will soon be moving over the Rio Grande Valley. The northern edge of the warm air will extend to the Dakotas and Minnesota, but the warming will be tempered in areas covered by a significant amount of snow. With as much as three feet of fresh powder on the ground in parts of northeast Minnesota and northern Wisconsin, warm air will have difficulty gaining a foothold in the northern

Great Lakes region."

All this talk of high pressures and low pressures was sending the Rebbe's internal barometer soaring. He had to find some way to steer the forecaster eastward. The next breathing pause allowed him time for only one word: "BOSTON!"

"Certainly," the weatherologist responded. "The storm system that spawned powerful thunderstorms in southwestern New England and heavy snow in parts of Rhode Island will gain in potency as it derives more energy from the confrontation of the cold- and warm-air fronts. Northeast winds will average 25 to 35 knots and tonight will remain windy, unseasonably cold and overcast, with high- and middle-level clouds."

By this time the Rebbe wasn't sure if there would *be* any weather on Wednesday. He asked Woltersdorf if he knew what time daybreak would occur.

"The moon rises at 7:32 A.M., and sets at 10:02 P.M.," the fellow chimed monotonously. "Saturn rises at 2:57 A.M., and sets at 12:17 P.M. Jupiter rises at 9:20 A.M., and sets at 11:47 P.M. Mars rises at 9:09 A.M., and sets at 11:53 P.M. Venus rises at 6:09 A.M., and sets at 5:21 P.M...."

Fortunately the Rebbe was able to arrest him before he completed the astronomy lesson. Marvin still had several planets to go and who knew how many trenchant details and cogent facts germane to constellations and planetary satellites he would consider essential to the presentation.

"Dr. Woltersdorf," the Rabbi pleaded, unable to keep the note of desperation from his voice, "could you please just tell me in the simplest English whether or not the sun will be visible early Wednesday morning?"

"Why didn't you say that in the first place?" he replied indignantly, somewhat taken aback that his audience was less than appreciative of his very thorough and erudite recitation. "I would say that the likelihood is infinitesimal."

The Rebbe thanked Woltersdorf for his time. It was a good thing, he mused, that he'd asked the scientist to phrase his response in simple English.

WITH GREAT TREPIDATION, the Rebbe realized that he had to activate "Plan B." The year was 1953, and like most other civilians in that era of commercial aviation's infancy, he had never flown before. "Well, there's no time like the present," he told himself.

Leibel, his dialing finger poised, awaited instructions. "Call a travel agency, please," the Rebbe requested, "and ask for the shortest flight available out of Logan Airport." Wattstein hastened to comply.

When the travel agent answered and began to speak to Leibel, he immediately sensed he was dealing with a novice. Bent on landing a sizable commission, he launched into a lengthy excursus about options and destinations, and Leibel had trouble keeping up. "We have one short flight," the agent began, "which includes deluxe hotel accommodations for two. Alternatively, you can substitute car rental for hotel reservations. For a small additional charge, a tour guide and chauffeured limousine can pick you up at the airport terminal…"

The Rebbe quickly cut off Leibel's reiteration of the agent's spiel. After an entire morningful of Cal Lacy and Marvin Woltersdorf, he had little patience for a recital of the complete itinerary for his "dream vacation." "Just ask him," the Rebbe said, "what is the shortest and cheapest flight, one-way, out of Boston."

After a good deal of page-shuffling, the agent reported that the cheapest fare, and also the shortest route, was from Logan to New York's Idlewild Airport. "However," he quickly added, "for just an extra $30 you can fly on to Philly, where there is a marvelous exhibition opening in the science museum…"

The Rebbe requested a reservation on the first Wednesday morning flight to New York. "The one that takes off just before sunrise, please. No return flight, no hotel reservations, and no car rentals!"

"How about a booking on the Circle Line sightseeing tour of Manhattan?" the agent countered. "And you'll certainly want me to book you tickets for some Broadway shows."

Leibel looked at the Rebbe expectantly, but the Rebbe shook his head. "No, thank you," Leibel told the agent, "just the airline ticket."

"All right," the man said, his tone resigned. "But don't blame me if they only let ticket-holders into *Bwana Devil*. And there's a performance of 'How Much is That Doggie in the Window' at Radio City, and unless you order a ticket now, the only way you'll get into a 3-D movie is by paying triple the price to the scalpers…"

"How much is the one-way ticket to New York, without movies, and without the 'Doggie in the Window'?" Leibel asked.

"That's fifty-two dollars, plus sales tax, and you'll have to come down to our office tomorrow to pick it up. While you're here, I'll show you our new travel brochure on the

Bahamas. The islands are totally unspoiled by civilization, and we have a special rate…"

WEDNESDAY MORNING the Rebbe arose very early for the flight. A gelatinous pea soup was brewing outside the window, clearly vindicating his efforts and expense to evade the weather. But excited as he was about performing this special *mitzvah*, he was equally apprehensive about flying. From all that he'd heard, it could be a harrowing experience.

Should he take along ear plugs? he wondered, or medicine to counteract air sickness? He was hesitant to phone the few experienced flyers he knew, lest they arouse his fears instead of allaying them. All the way to the airport, the words of a radio report he'd heard about a zeppelin that burst into flames echoed loudly in his head. Could that happen to a four-engine turbo?

Check-in was blessedly uneventful, and not all that different from the routine at the Greyhound Bus Terminal. It was outside on the tarmac that reality struck full force, with new sights, sounds, and smells. The plane was enormous, and the Rebbe couldn't fathom how they would get it into the air. He tried to take solace in the fact that all of the other passengers about to board were entirely unexcited, even nonchalant, and were either glancing at the *Boston Globe* or conversing calmly with their fellow flyers. Apparently he was the only tyro.

The Talmud avers that a *mitzvah* emissary will not be harmed. At different times and under different circumstances these words undoubtedly brought peace of mind to Jews traveling the pirate-infested high seas, *shtadlanim* en route to meet with a local *poritz*, and a host of other journeyers in hazardous situations. The Rebbe drew comfort from the Talmudic guarantee: only the overwhelming desire to perform this *mitzvah* could have brought him to board that awesome behemoth.

Contemplating the words of the Sages, the Rebbe tried to calm himself and prepare for the moment of a lifetime. He considered which side of the plane would afford him the better view of the sun, and made sure to get a seat near the window, a spot he intended never to choose again unless he were faced with the same *Birkas Ha-chammah* dilemma in the future.

The propellers began to rotate dizzyingly and then, as if on cue, the passengers all strapped themselves into unwieldy shoulder- and waist-harnesses. The plane started taxiing and the Rebbe gave *tefillas ha-derech* everything he had.

As the plane made its way down the runway, the engine began to roar. With a drawn-out, ear-shattering screech, the monster raced to liftoff and the Rebbe's heart raced to his feet. At that moment he became convinced that never would he be a member of the *frum* jet set.

The ride, confounded no doubt by the blustery weather, was disconcertingly turbulent. A pamphlet of special *Birkas Ha-chammah tefillos* in hand, and nearly breathless with anticipation, the Rebbe kept his eyes riveted to the window, waiting for the plane to ascend above the clouds. But instead of climbing over the weather, the plane more or less leveled off, and for nearly half an hour maintained its course through the overcast skies. The Rebbe became very agitated. All of his efforts had been for naught, he thought;

50. The Satmar Rebbe, *center*, visiting with the Rebbe in Miami Beach, Florida, 1985.

51. The Rebbe and a group of students from Givat Pinchas draw the *mayim shelanu* before Passover from a well in Beit Tzefafa,

52. The Rebbe's appearance at the funeral of Yosef Gadish
    turned many a bare head. What possible connection could
    there have been between the distinguished leader of the
    Bostoner *chassidim*, and a stalwart of Mapai — a political party
    noted for its socialist/Marxist values and policies antithetical
    to Torah?

    The Rebbe explained that Yosef Gadish, in his capacity as
    Deputy Mayor of Jerusalem, had been instrumental in giving
    the Boston community its foothold in the Har Nof
    neighborhood of Jerusalem.

    It all began in the summer of 1983, at the *sheva berachos* of
    a Jerusalem family who had had some contact with the
    Chassidic Center in Boston. The Rebbe was introduced to
    Gadish there and the two hit it off very well.

    A few weeks later, as the Rebbe was preparing to return to
    America after a somewhat fruitless seed trip for the Har Nof
    Boston community, he decided to call Mr. Gadish as a gesture
    of courtesy, to say goodbye. To the Rebbe's surprise Gadish
    told him that he must see him right away.

    "I wish I could accommodate you..." the Rebbe said, "but
    I'm leaving for the States tomorrow evening."

    "Well, then, there's still plenty of time," Gadish responded.
    "I would come to see you, but I have meetings in my office all
    day. Please try and be here by seven tonight."

    Something in the tone of Gadish's voice urged the Rebbe to
    comply. When he walked into his seven o'clock meeting he
    found the Deputy Mayor animated and extremely friendly.
    Gadish told him that he had just read a most impressive
    newspaper article about the work the Rebbe does to help the
    infirm. He had also heard from a friend who had undergone
    extensive medical treatment in Boston and who was full of

praise for the Rebbe's and R.O.F.E.H.'s assistance.

"Now," Gadish declared, "I would like to see how I can help you. Tell me, how are the plans for your community developing?"

In truth they were undeveloped, or perhaps better expressed, needed quite a lot of development. A chassidic community without a *shul* was patently absurd, but despite all of the Rebbe's meetings and explorations during his visit to Israel, no progress had been made in this area. The Rebbe, chagrined over having nothing to report, responded instead with a more face-saving, "We are negotiating."

"And how about the *shul*?"

The question took the Rebbe by surprise. The *shul* was the crux of the entire project! The thought that someone in a position of influence might now be taking an interest ignited the Rebbe's imagination and rekindled his hopes. As nonchalantly as he could, he replied, "Why, that is *your* domain."

The Deputy Mayor nodded and said, "I'll give you a *shul*. The cost of building one, and I'm referring to the real cost — no frills — is $150,000, with the infrastructure and land rights thrown in by us. Give us a third and it's yours."

The Rebbe was absolutely flabbergasted. Yes, yes, of course the answer was yes, he wanted the *shul* with all his heart. This was the windfall he had prayed for. The glorious dream of settling Boston in Israel was about to come true — but there was one hitch: the family tradition. The Rebbe's father, in his day, would not move into a neighborhood unless there was a *mikveh* there, even if that entailed constructing one on his own. Could the Rebbe have the audacity to ask his new-found friend, who was already offering him so much, for *mikveh* facilities as well? But then again, could he not?

As diplomatically as possible, the Rebbe explained that although he was most grateful for the exceedingly generous offer, a *shul* without a *mikveh* was out of the question.

Gadish seemed sympathetic but his response was negative: there was no room on the site for a *mikveh* as well as a *shul*. "It needn't be a big *mikveh*," the Rebbe urged, "just a *mikveh*."

Gadish grabbed the phone and got his engineer on the line. A fast-paced discussion took place, and arrangements were made for the engineer to go to the site the following morning, meet with the Rebbe, and look into the possibility of construcing a *mikveh* on the same plot as the *shul*.

Two hours before check-in time for the Rebbe's return flight to the States, a suitable location for the *mikveh* was indeed discovered and the engineering feasibility worked out, but unless a contract was signed within the next 45 minutes, all the efforts would have been in vain. When the Rebbe would next visit Israel, this prime property would surely have been allocated to someone else. The Rebbe and Dr. Moshe Singer, general manager of Boston-Jerusalem, sped to Gadish's office with their pens poised — they had to seal this deal NOW!

The Rebbe made a somewhat uncharacteristic entrance into Gadish's office, an exuberant expression on his face. *"Mazel und bracha!"* he exclaimed. "The deal is on!"

The Rebbe pulled a spare *kippah* from his pocket for the Deputy Mayor, to insure that this moment would be consummated in the appropriate atmosphere, but Gadish declined the Rebbe's offer. Reaching into his closet, Gadish produced a *kippah* of his *own*. Then, insisting that the Rebbe be seated in his executive chair, he arranged the papers on the desk for all to sign.

With the signing completed and a round of *L'chaims* toasted for the auspicious occasion, the Deputy Mayor rose from his seat, embraced the Rebbe and planted a kiss on his cheek. "I love you!" he said, and the Rebbe warmly returned his embrace.

A year later, when Yosef Gadish passed away, not only did the Rebbe attend the funeral, but he instructed his *kollel* to recite *Kaddish* and learn *mishnayos* for one year in Gadish's memory. "Because of this man," the Rebbe declared, "thousands of people have a beautiful *shul* and *beis midrash* to learn and *daven* in all day and all night."

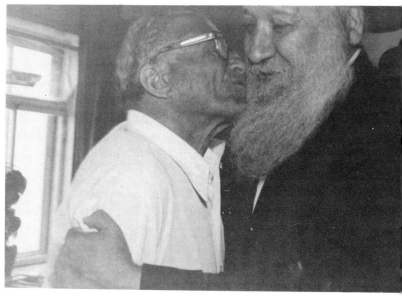

53. Givat Pinchas, the center of Bostoner *chassidus* in Har Nof.

54. At the *Chanukas Ha-bayis* of Givat Pinchas. *Left to right,* Rav
Shalom Mashash, Sephardi Chief Rabbi of Jerusalem;
[unidentified]; R. Yehuda Tzadkah, *Rosh Yeshiva* of Porat
Yosef; the Rebbe; the *Rishon L'Tzion,* R. Mordechai Eliyahu,
Sephardi Chief Rabbi of Israel (speaking); R. Shlomo Neiman,
Rav of the Border Police and of Ramot; R. Yitzchak Kolitz,
Ashkenazi Chief Rabbi of Jerusalem.

55. At the *Chanukas Ha-bayis* for Givat Pinchas, 1985, the Rebbe received the blessing of R. Shlomo Zalman Auerbach.

56. R. Yitzhak Kolitz, Ashkenazi Chief Rabbi of Jerusalem, joined in the *Chanukas Ha-bayis* celebrations.

57. The Rebbe with R. Moshe Hagar, the Vishnitzer Rebbe, at the *Chanukas Ha-bayis*.

58. Rav Yosef Sholom Elyashiv, renowned Jerusalem *posek*, visits with the Rebbe on the occasion of the *Chanukas Ha-bayis* of Givat Pinchas.

59. The Rebbe with Rav Eliezer Mann Shach, the *Rosh Yeshiva* of Ponovezh, while attending the *Chanukas Ha-bayis*.

60. The Rebbe greeting IDF soldiers at the Western Wall.

he was about to miss the opportunity of a lifetime.

In desperation he signaled the flight attendant, who was busy dishing out some kind of soup from a thermos. The stewardess negotiated her way to his seat and prepared to pour the Rebbe some clam chowder which he naturally refused. Shouting above the din of the engines, the Rebbe asked her to explain to the captain that he was on a special mission. "I must get above the clouds," he urged, "even if only for a moment."

The startled stewardess eyed him closely, taking in the Rebbe's garb, his flowing beard and sidelocks. She could not deny the earnestness of this unusual passenger's pleas. She told the Rebbe that as soon as she finished serving the meal she would convey his message to the flight deck.

The Rebbe waited impatiently for mealtime to end and the stewardess to keep her promise. Eventually she did enter the cockpit, but only for a moment. She rushed right out, threw the curtain closed, and strapped on her seat belt.

Moments later the plane began to vibrate and undulate. The Rebbe's eyes were still fixed on the window, but the view was far from enjoyable. Clutching the arms of his seat tightly, he prayed fervently for mercy. True, *Birkas Ha-chammah* is an important *mitzvah*, he told himself, but one is not required to jeopardize his life in order to fulfill it!

It was obvious that before the stewardess could possibly have relayed the Rebbe's request to the captain, he had ordered her to take her seat because the plane was entering a patch of heavy air disturbance. Now the opportunity was lost. The brief journey was almost over and they would soon be landing in New York, without ever having glimpsed the sun. From his vantage point, the Rebbe didn't

need Dr. Woltersdorf to tell him that the weather in the
New York area wasn't any better than in Massachusetts. He
was heartbroken.

Suddenly the plane seemed to gain altitude. A solid wall
of what appeared to be dark cotton candy engulfed it and
then, for just a fleeting second, it surfaced above the cloud
layer. Blinding light filled the cabin and the Rebbe quickly
recited that magnificent blessing: "*Oseh ma'asei Bereshis* —
Who performs the wonders of Creation."

The sun had never looked more resplendent, its rays
shimmering off the plane's silver wings in a glorious spectrum of color. An instant after the Rebbe uttered the final
word of the *berachah*, the plane reentered the clouds and
began its descent into Idlewild.

The Rebbe was ecstatic, elated with joy. Relief, triumph
and exultation mingled with a very spiritual sense of lofti-
ness and sublimity. The twenty-eight-year cycle and global
weather conditions conspire to deny many this precious
opportunity, yet God in His Kindness had enabled him to
perform the *mitzvah*, a *mitzvah* which he did not know if he
would ever perform again in his lifetime.

Author's note: In the *zechus* of his efforts to fulfill this
mitzvah, the Rebbe says, he was privileged to recite the
Birkas Ha-chammah twenty-eight years later, in 1981. But
that's another story.

What Will People Think!

L ate one spring night, just as the Rebbe was about to retire, there was an unnerving knock on his door. Always-available Leibel Wattstein was for once unavailable to tell the solicitor to try again in the morning, so the Rebbe tended to the matter himself.

Standing on the doorstep was a religious woman, whom the Rebbe did not recognize on sight, with a teenaged boy in tow. "Please forgive me for disturbing you at this hour," she said. "Could I possibly see you for just a few moments?" The Rebbe could tell from her tone that the matter was urgent. He ushered them into his study.

When they were seated, the woman introduced herself as Rebbetzin M., and the Rebbe realized that she was the wife of a famous *Rosh Yeshiva* from New York. The young man at her side, he gathered, was their son. One look was all the Rebbe needed; immediately he felt sorry for the woman. The boy had not uttered a word, but his arrogant demeanor spoke volumes. His hat was perched rakishly on his crown, his jacket draped casually over his shoulders, and two packs of cigarettes were jammed into his shirt pocket. The boy's face mirrored a sense of profound disdain.

Shlomo, Rebbetzin M. related, had been attending a yeshiva in the area up until a few hours earlier, when he was summarily evicted from the dorm. The administration would permit him to continue learning there provided he no longer slept in the dormitory, or remained on the premises after dark.

Of course that was tantamount to expulsion, but taking the boy's esteemed family into consideration, the administration preferred to word it in this convoluted way. Shlomo's mother, however, still considered the Boston yeshiva a viable option for her son and had therefore come to ask the Rebbe to provide lodging. It was clear to him that her request was based on the fact that no New York yeshiva would accept the boy, and this caused the Rebbe some concern. He could think of several possible reasons, none of them pleasant.

Ultimately the decision to admit the boy was motivated by a single factor: the Chassidic Center is home to everyone, from hippies to medical emergency cases to itinerant fund-raisers. It was only right, therefore, that the Rebbe should open his doors to a boarder from such a distinguished home. He also figured that with so many people staying with them, one more would hardly make a difference.

But he was mistaken. Sorely mistaken.

SHLOMO WAS a spoiled, insolent problem child. Nothing was good enough for him and everything had to be done precisely his way. The Rebbetzin and other residents of the Chassidic Center insisted that the Rebbe put his foot down and demand that Shlomo comport himself as a guest should, but the Rebbe hesitated. He sensed intuitively that strictness was not the way to reach this boy. One or two more wrong moves in Shlomo's education and development, and he might be lost entirely to *Yiddishkeit*.

Once the Rebbe established the policy that Shlomo was to be left alone, it was observed by all, albeit grudgingly. The major inconvenience was to the Rebbetzin, who had to cater to the boy's ever-changing dietary likes and dislikes. He had a "thing" about cholesterol and at first demanded that his chicken be braised, then he switched to poached, then to seared, baked, fried, and finally to boiled. Later he went on the Pritiken Diet which was equally incompatible with a chassidic household. This was followed by Macrobiotics, which entailed periodic shipments of seaweed by Chinese delivery boys. In the end Shlomo settled on a strict regimen of straight junk food.

Not only were his gastronomic preferences problematic; they were well nigh impossible to implement. The schedule of his mealtimes seemed to be governed solely by what time the Rebbe's were not. Nonetheless the Rebbetzin catered to his every capricious whim, without once receiving a compliment or gesture of gratitude.

Shlomo's individualism was not restricted to his alimentary excesses; he displayed remarkable selectivity in the realm of roommates as well. Indeed his taste in living partners was so refined that no one seemed to suit him. Thus Shlomo enjoyed the unique status of being the only tenant in the Chassidic Center in a room by himself.

The Rebbe ended up making this concession too, as he continued to reason that the way to conquer this boy was through kindness. The Rebbe made a point, therefore, of always greeting him warmly and exchanging a few words with him every day.

The one thing the Rebbe found himself unable to go along with, however, were Shlomo's nighttime meanderings. Where he gallivanted every night the Rebbe dared not guess, and he felt it irresponsible to let so reckless a youth go out by himself in the dark. But when he broached the subject with Shlomo, it practically terminated their tenuous relationship. The boy stormed out in a fit of rage, exhibiting anything but a readiness to discuss his nocturnal perambulations. From then on the Rebbe took care to avoid this irksome subject, and prayed that Shlomo wouldn't get into serious trouble.

ONE FATEFUL NIGHT a cacophony of sirens and klaxons was heard crescendoing around the neighborhood. Leibel, the Chassidic Center's aging self-appointed security man, headed immediately for his favorite hideout — under one of the benches in the *shul* — while the Rebbe rushed to the window to see what the commotion was all about. Seconds later the Rebbetzin came hurrying to his side, drying her hands on her apron.

A flotilla of wailing squad cars with blue and red lights flashing was converging on...the Chassidic Center! From either end of Beacon and down the side street the cruisers sailed, screeching to a halt just below the Rebbe's window. The look of concern on the Rebbetzin's face matched her husband's. What would people think!

From the Rebbe's vantage point, the collection of squad cars parked half on the street, half on the sidewalk, and some abandoned in mid-gutter, looked like a bunch of Pick-up Stix, tossed willy-nilly. The car doors were flung open — and left open — and an army of patrolmen clad in blue came piling into the building.

The Rebbe's first thought was of Shlomo and his antics, and his stomach clenched with worry. He and the Rebbetzin rushed downstairs to find out what the police wanted, but the patrolmen wouldn't even stop to speak. All they said was "The roof, the roof!"

One of the cops finally discovered the staircase and signaled to his men. Like a graceless team of Russian weight lifters they trudged up the stairs to the beat of "The roof, the roof!" unholstering their revolvers as they climbed. Out of the corner of his eye, the Rebbe saw Leibel scamper to a more remote retreat as the Rebbetzin tried in vain to delay the intruders' progress by begging for an explanation. But the only response she received was "The roof, the roof!" — by now a familiar chant. The Rebbetzin, trailed by other residents of the Chassidic Center, followed the cops' ascent to the roof. It was a pathetic sight.

One patrolman who had been speaking into the police radio in his cruiser straggled in behind the others and the Rebbe managed to glean a few skimpy details out of this Johnny-come-lately. Apparently a neighbor had heard footsteps on her roof and called the already complaint-inundated police department to report a voyeur prowling the area. That was all the cop would reveal before adding his voice to the "The roof!" incantation.

The Rebbe's heart sank. He could just see the headlines:

"PIOUS PEEPING PINCUS," "HASSIDIC DEVIANT," "RELIGIOUS INQUIRER." He sent Leibel upstairs to check if Shlomo was in his room, but even before Wattstein came down huffing and puffing and scurrying back to his hiding place, the Rebbe knew the response would be negative.

Anxiously he awaited the cops' descent. Shouts of "Hey, over here!" and "What's that?" drifted down to him in the darkness as visions of his youthful charge being hauled off in handcuffs filled the Rebbe's mind. Pushing those terrible thoughts aside, he prayed it was not Shlomo who was the object of this manhunt, but knowing at the same time that it was.

At last the police trouped down the stairs...empty-handed. "Looks like we're black and blue tonight," a young patrolman commented, and then cringed as he realized his faux pas. His cronies slapped him on the back and squeezed his neck companionably, pushing him to the front of the line headed for the squad cars. Soon the whooping sirens and flashing lights were gone and the street was silent once more.

Leibel poked his head out from under his bench. "Is the coast clear?" he asked shakily. But before the Rebbe could reply, Shlomo sauntered in, whistling a lively tune.

Hands jammed in his pockets, the boy took in the strange scene. "What's up?" he asked as everyone gawked at him wordlessly.

"Everything's fine now," the Rebbe said, berating himself inwardly for the miscarriage of justice that had taken place in the courtrooms of his mind.

A popular public service advertisement of the time challenged: "It's ten o'clock — do you know where your children are?" The Rebbe had even quoted that adage in one of his sermons about *chinnuch*, and now those words came back to haunt him. "Here I am, a sort of surrogate father to this boy," he chastised himself, "and I have absolutely no idea where he is night after night." True, it was not the Rebbe's job to be a babysitter, but still he felt morally responsible for Shlomo's well-being. The fact that Shlomo wasn't the Peeping Tom was faint consolation.

After the tension of the preceding half-hour, the Rebbe was too agitated to even greet the peripatetic youth. The Rebbetzin, however, quickly regained her composure and welcomed her young boarder. "You missed all the action!" she called cheerfully.

When the Rebbetzin told him what had transpired, Shlomo's face turned crimson with embarrassment. "How low can you go?" he railed at the unknown felon. "Peering into people's windows?! That's...that's contemptible!" He shook his head back and forth in disgust.

The kid's stocks were rising: he wasn't the culprit, hadn't sullied the reputation of the Chassidic Center, and his sense of moral outrage was intact. The Rebbe felt proud of the boy...until Shlomo unloaded the bombshell: As calmly as a spectator watching grass grow, he announced that he had been the person on the roof.

The Rebbe's jaw dropped.

"But I didn't see any 'Peeping Tom' up there," Shlomo added hastily. "There was no one there but me —" Suddenly the boy's face paled as he realized the implication of his statement. "You don't think *I*...!"

The Rebbe made a tremendous effort to control his

temper. Thank God, the Chassidic Center had been spared the bad P.R., but now it seemed the Rebbe's initial suspicions had been right on the mark.

It was clear to the Rebbe that he had been far too lax with Shlomo and had allowed the boy's capers to get out of hand. Shlomo, he was now convinced, needed a strong, rather than a gentle hand. Before releasing the strident tirade which welled up inside him, the Rebbe decided to give Shlomo an opportunity to explain and justify his apparently prurient behavior. "What were you doing on the roof?" he demanded.

There was a long silence before Shlomo responded. Mutely he stared at the floor, his shoulders slumped in despair. But when he raised his head at last, he looked the Rebbe squarely in the eye and spoke in a firm, confident voice that for once was free of arrogance. "Before I explain," he said, "I want to apologize to you and the Rebbetzin. I had no intention, no intention whatsoever, of creating a public spectacle when I went out on the roof. I gave no thought at all to the possible consequences, but if I had, I don't believe I would have acted any differently. It was almost, no, it *was* a compulsion — I *had* to go up there. In fact, I've been up there every single night since my arrival."

The Rebbe gasped. What peril this boy, for whom the Rebbe was responsible, had subjected himself to — not once, but again, and again, and again! He braced himself for the revelation that was to come.

"I have been going out on the roof for one reason only: to escape, to escape the scrutiny of other people. I have to get away from where people watch my every act, criticize my every word, and compare me to my older brothers and brothers-in-law. It seems it just never occurred to anyone that with a father who is a brilliant *Rosh Yeshiva* and brothers who are diligent, outstanding students, that I might be any different. But the fact is that I am.

"When my brothers were growing up, my father was still a *Gemara rebbe*. No one in the neighborhood cared very much what the rebbe's boys did, and so they had a more or less normal childhood. They played ball with their classmates during recess, went to summer camp, even got into a little mischief once in a while.

"But I am the *ben zekunim*. By the time I was three my father was recognized as one of the 'nifty fifty,' my brothers were the stars of their yeshivas, and my brothers-in-law were their only equals.

"Isn't it only natural, then, that I should be a little angel? Every move I ever made was reported in great detail to my father, who forever lectured me on setting the right example, on not bringing shame to his house. Play ball with the guys? Heaven forfend! What if I fell and tore my clothes — what would people think if they saw the *Rosh Yeshiva*'s kid walking around in tatters, or with dirt on his face?! What would people think, what would people think..."

"Shlomo," the Rebbe interrupted, "what does this have to do with looking into neighbors' windows?"

"Looking into neighbors' windows? *Chalilah!* I didn't look into anybody's windows — I wouldn't do that! I was looking at the sky...

"When I went up on the roof tonight I had the thrill of my life. The air was so crisp, and the breeze so refreshing. The night was starry and it seemed like I could see for miles. It was so great standing up there all by myself, without anyone watching me, without anyone even knowing where I was.

"I worked up the nerve to inch over to the edge of the roof. Until tonight, I hadn't had the courage to do that. And when I peered over the parapet, it seemed as if I were standing directly above the neighbor's roof. I was overcome with an urge to do something I had never, ever, done before."

Long seconds passed before Shlomo continued: "I took off my jacket and climbed over the parapet and onto the ledge. Then, carefully measuring the distance with my eyes, I held my breath and…jumped. It was so cool! It was like flying! The wind whipped my hair back, my clothes pressed against me like a second skin, and my heart pounded like a jackhammer!

"But I couldn't just stop there; the experience was exhilirating. I began leaping like a cat from rooftop to rooftop, all over the whole neighborhood, until I found one low enough to jump down to the street.

"Now Rebbe, I know what you're going to say, that it's *asur* to risk my life, but I just couldn't resist the temptation. You see, it wasn't just the achievement of the jump that thrilled me, it was the *freedom!* For once in my life I was free to be a child. That's pretty ironic, coming from someone who spent his childhood behaving like a perfect adult.

"A *Rosh Yeshiva*'s son, my father always said, does not get into mischief. When I would protest that *yenner*'s and *plony*'s sons were allowed, my father would respond that *I* was destined to follow in his footsteps. Of course this meant that *I* was *not* allowed. Well, tonight I allowed *myself*, and I'm prepared to face the consequences. Whatever they are, it was worth it."

The Rebbe somberly reflected on what Shlomo had said about never having had the chance to be a child, even when he was an exuberant youngster. From the time of his birth, his father had expected him to behave as if he were already a *Rosh Yeshiva*. The words of Shlomo's namesake echoed in the Rebbe's mind: "Educate the child according to his needs," the wise king advised, "then even when he grows old he will not digress."

Placing a gentle hand on Shlomo's shoulder, the Rebbe said, "I understand, my son. But now I hope all of this is behind you. Now it's time to begin to truly fulfill your destiny."

Author's note: He did.

The Mystery of the Moribund Meshulach

The sky over Boston that day was the color of wet newspaper, and the usual sidewalk litter huddled beneath a pristine blanket of fresh snow. The wind howled with a premonitory echo and strong, frigid gusts rattled the shutters of 17-10 Beacon Street as if to intimate that tragedy was in the air. When the phone call came bearing bad tidings, the Rebbe was not surprised.

Mrs. Morgan was on the line, frantic with grief and anxiety. Ordinarily poised and levelheaded, Betty Morgan was not a woman given to histrionics. Clearly something was terribly wrong. The Rebbe urged her to calm down and tell him what had happened.

About a jubilee ago, the Morgans had moved to the West End of Boston, where they opened the only *shomer Shabbos* grocery in town. Their standard of *kashrus* was trustworthy, their prices fair, and service friendly. They were active in community affairs and always among the first to volunteer their assistance when the need arose. Even after her husband's passing, Betty continued to be involved in *chessed*. If there was a *mitzvah* to perform or an unpleasant task to carry out, Betty Morgan could always be relied upon.

Mrs. Morgan's most outstanding virtue was her *hachnasas orchim*. Her home had been transformed into a veritable inn, second only to the Chassidic Center in the number of wayfarers it housed. It was understood that if the Rebbe's home was booked to capacity, guests could always be referred to the Morgans.

Among her regulars were a host of *meshulachim* and this was the reason for her call: one such guest did not wake up this morning. A doctor had been called in and the *meshulach* was pronounced dead, but before the *Chevrah Kadisha* arrived, the body was carted off to the city morgue, and Mrs. Morgan didn't even know his name! She could find nothing among his belongings — not even his receipt book — with his name on it, and no way to identify him.

The police informed her that if no one came to claim the body within 48 hours, it would be officially designated a "John Doe" and eventually interred in a potter's field.

Remarkably, Mrs. Morgan did not know the first thing about this man, save his dietary likes and dislikes and the fact that the police pathologist estimated his age to be 93. He had stayed at her home several times over the years, but had lived reclusively and was loath to talk about himself, and she, of course, had never pried.

The Rebbe saw that there was little point in pressing Betty for information which she did not have, but meanwhile this mystery had to be solved, and the corpse transferred from the city morgue to Jewish auspices without delay.

The Rebbe phoned the Police Department and spoke to an officer with whom he'd worked in the past. He presented the halachic dilemma and tried to impress upon the officer the urgency of moving the body to a Jewish funeral parlor where a *shomer* could award the *niftar* the respect he deserved.

Unimpressed, the police were not prepared to deviate from standard regulations. The officer explained that it was unlawful and unprecedented to remove a corpse from the morgue without the written consent of family. "Afraid I can't help you, Rabbi," he said.

Although the Rebbe had always prided himself on being a law-abiding citizen, he realized that this was not a time to defer to civic legalities; the sanctity of a Jewish body was at stake. In his zeal to conform with the dictates of *Halachah*, the Rebbe made a bold and rather hasty assertion: "If you will agree to release the body," he assured the officer, "I will undertake to solve the identity mystery."

To his amazement, the overworked Brookline Police Department readily gave their consent.

The problem, however, was far from solved. Now the Rebbe had to deal with the even more complex dilemma of finding out whose body it was that they were transferring. He rose from his desk and settled into his wing chair to consider a course of action. This was clearly a case for "*Reb* Sherlock."

As the Rebbe contemplated the pitifully few angles there were to pursue, his trusty assistant, Leibel Wattstein, entered and sensed immediately that something was troubling his mentor.

"What's the matter, Rebbe?" he asked.

"Leibel," the Rebbe said, "how would you trace the identity of a 93-year-old itinerant loner? Male, Caucasian, average weight, 5′5″ tall, wearing a long black coat and trousers, white shirt, no tie?"

"Did you try asking him?" Leibel suggested with a youthful exuberance that belied his years.

"I'm afraid he's dead," the Rebbe replied, foregoing the opportunity to engage in black humor.

"Oy, I'm sorry, Rebbe…Maybe there were some witnesses at the scene of the crime?"

"There was no crime, my friend. An old man simply did not wake up in the morning."

"Oh. In that case, *baruch Dayan Ha-Emes*." Leibel's mobile face contorted into an appropriate expression of sorrow. After a decent interval, he brightened. "Sounds like a real mystery, Rebbe," he said enthusiastically. "Are there any other clues?"

"Not a one," the Rebbe replied. He pondered another moment, then signaled for Leibel to bring him the telephone. It had occurred to him that in the course of soliciting funds, the *meshulach* might have revealed some information about himself, so he decided to do some checking.

According to Betty Morgan, the *meshulach* did most of his soliciting in the Chelsea neighborhood, but the Rebbe's initial phone calls to acquaintances in that area failed to turn up any leads. The Rebbe then dispatched Leibel to pound the streets of Chelsea, to see what he could come up with, and resumed his pondering pose.

A good four hours later, when a frustrated Leibel Wattstein returned to the Chassidic Center and found the

Rebbe poring over a *sefer*, his countenance became a mask of incredulity. "Rebbe!" he exclaimed, innocently over-stepping the bounds of propriety. "How can you learn at a time like this? What about our emergency?"

"Oh, that," the Rebbe said casually, as though the mystery of the moribund *meshulach* were ancient history. "That's all taken care of."

"What?!" Leibel cried.

"I tried to get hold of you in Chelsea," the Rebbe said, "but was unsuccessful."

Unable to contain his curiosity, Leibel stammered in stupefaction. "Rebbe, what...er, how...uh, when...eh, *who?*"

The Rebbe motioned for Leibel to take a seat and related the entire saga.

"Shortly after you left," he began, "I remembered that Harry Silver lives in Chelsea and, may he live and be well, he always makes it his business to know everyone's business. A man of means, Harry would inevitably be included on any charity collector's solicitation route. I was certain our mystery *meshulach* had not overlooked him.

"No one, no matter how introverted, can withstand Harry's interrogations. It's not that Silver is nosy; he's simply fascinated by people, and they always respond to his gentle questioning because they recognize the sincerity behind it. I knew that even this taciturn fund-raiser could not have left the Silver household without revealing at least some details about his background.

"I got Harry on the phone and he conceded that our *meshulach* had indeed been a very hard nut to crack. The one and only thing Harry had been able to get out of him was that he hailed from Williamsburg, near the site of the old Torah Vodaath Yeshiva. Well, that limited the possibilities to about a ten-block radius, an area which I estimate contains approximately seventeen thousand Jews."

Leibel swallowed hard. "Why, that didn't make it much easier," he protested.

"Of course it did, my friend," the Rebbe said with a smile. "How many 93-year-old introverted *meshulachim* do you think come from that area? Not many, I assure you. I then called directory assistance and asked them for the listing of Goldberg on Clymer Street, a heavily populated residential area adjacent to Torah Vodaath."

"Whew, Rebbe," Leibel sighed with relief. "What *mazel* it was that you knew someone in the area."

"I didn't," the Rebbe said, motioning for Leibel to keep his comments to a minimum. "I figured there must be at least one Goldberg listed, and this Goldberg might know our *meshulach*.

"The operator had little patience; she said there were too many Goldbergs listed for her to verify the street address without getting a first name. So I told her I was looking for 'Mordechai' Goldberg on Clymer."

"Why *Mordechai*?" Leibel asked, missing the Rebbe's train of thought.

"*Mordechai*," the Rebbe explained patiently, "because anyone who retains such a difficult name for non-Jews to pronounce, without anglicizing it to Murray or Morton or Whatever, must be unabashedly and unself-consciously Jewish. Such a person, I thought, was likely to know the name of the *meshulach* — and of course he did: it was Fleishman.

"I had a very pleasant conversation with Mordechai Goldberg — it turns out I once did his brother-in-law a favor. I did not hesitate to cash in, and asked him if he could look up the *meshulach*'s phone number for me in the Brooklyn phone book.

"He told me that there were no Williamsburg listings for 'Fleishman,' and then he recalled a rumor that the man had moved out of the neighborhood. He read me the addresses of the other Fleishmans in Brooklyn, and together we immediately eliminated all those living in affluent areas of the borough. Since neither of us knew the man's first name, we had to guess which address was the most likely.

"I rejected the Bensonhurst, Canarsie, and two Flatbush candidates, and opted instead for the sole Fleishman listed in Crown Heights, one Thelma Fleishman."

"What made you choose that one, Rebbe?" Leibel asked.

"I don't know," the Rebbe replied. "I can only say that the Almighty directed my choice, although at first I was sure I had dialed the wrong number."

A middle-aged woman had answered the phone. As soon as the Rebbe related that he was trying to find out about an elderly Fleishman, there was a rush of disclaimers about knowing anything of the individual in question.

There was something about this woman's emphatic denials, however, that aroused the Rebbe's suspicions. He gathered he was not the first caller to bother Ms. Fleishman about the nonagenarian's activities. After assuring her that he was *not* trying to collect any money owed to him, or even to discover the *meshulach*'s whereabouts, the Rebbe identified himself and told Ms. Fleishman that he had to contact the elderly gentleman's family right away as he was the bearer of bad tidings.

The woman at the other end of the line fell silent. "Bad tidings?" she asked at last, and confessed to being the deceased's daughter. The Rebbe asked her to describe her father's appearance, and everything she said matched what he had been told about the *meshulach*.

It wasn't until after she finished describing the man, that the Rebbe informed her that her father had passed away. Ms. Fleishman did not reply but soon the Rebbe heard the sound of sobbing.

To his unending sorrow, the Rebbe, numerous times in the past, has had the unpleasant task of informing people of their parents' demise. Now he drew upon experience to try to comfort Ms. Fleishman long-distance, and at the same time instruct her as to how she should proceed. The first priority was to hire a limousine to bring the body to New York for burial.

AS THE REBBE was describing the final steps of the drama, the phone rang and Leibel ran to answer it. "It's for you Rebbe," he said.

The Rebbe instructed him to put it on the speaker-phone and a gruff voice came over the line. "Rabbi Horowitz, this is Lieutenant Roger O'Shea, Chief of Detectives, Brookline Police Department. I just wanted to congratulate you! I don't know how you did it. I've been on the squad for twenty-three years, and I can't remember a single John Doe case like this that we've cracked, even with ten times the evidence you had.

"If you ever want a job, Rabbi, we've got a desk right

here, ready and waiting for you."

"Thank you very much, Lieutenant," the Rebbe said, "but for the time being I prefer to stay at my present position. The hours are long, but there's a great deal of job satisfaction. If I ever change my mind I'll let you know."

Leibel was obviously impressed. "Rebbe," he said, "that really was a great piece of detective work. How did you know just what to do?"

The Rebbe sank back in his chair, slid his "thinking cap" forward, and with a straight face replied, "Elementary, my dear Wattstein."

Epilogue

The preceding is but a glimpse of the struggles, the drama, the sorrows and joys that comprise the life of any Jewish communal leader. Rabbi Levi Yitzchak Horowitz, however, is not a typical Jewish communal leader by any standard. Through his teachings and example, tens of thousands of our People have been inspired to maintain a more observant life style, to strengthen their commitment to the Land of Israel, and to reach out to their brethren in need.

To the conventional methods of conveying these vital lessons, the Rebbe has added another, most crucial factor: his presence. His very presence, deportment and attire have themselves had an impact on the lives of untold individuals. At times it is subtle; at times profound.

The Sages tell us that our forefathers merited redemption from Egyptian bondage because they retained their sacred language, their Hebrew names and their distinctive attire. The lesson to be learned from this is clear: If one not only adheres to Torah Law, but dresses and conducts himself in a manner distinct from his Gentile neighbors, the impression, as "Melissa Paine" poignantly writes below, is indelible and the implications far-reaching. This personal letter has been included in this volume in the hope that, like the pages which precede it, it will serve to inspire others to attempt to touch the lives of their coreligionists, wherever they may be.

Hello — finally — to "Grand Rabbi Horowitz"!

I grew up in Weston, Massachusetts and my summer months were spent at my Grandmother Cele's house on Sunset Avenue in Nantasket Beach.

*There are many vivid images I still reflect on from those summers. I remember little Mikey Fox, Myra and Herbert Fox's son, who always acted very peculiarly. I remember the way he'd ride his bike aimlessly, up and down the street. I remember how he would shake the hand of everyone who came within a ten-foot radius of him. I remember how gentle he was and how terrified he became whenever the sea rose to the second bar of the white picket fence that ran along the shoreline. It was frightening for me, too, when the tide rose, and especially frightening when a storm was brewing. As a little girl, I often wished I was Mikey when the tide flooded in like that. I too wanted to cry, to scream as he did, to express my fear openly, but I could not. That was not the role I was meant to play. Although I was younger than he was, I understood even then that I had a responsibility to myself and to those around me to behave appropriately — not so much because I **had** to, but because, unlike Mikey, I **could**.*

I recently attended a week-long Jewish Discovery Program and I equate the story above with the way I felt at the end of that week. I felt frightened and overwhelmed by what I had learned. I wanted to forget everything I'd heard, or to scream and shout and make it all go away. But how does one with a vital mind forget what she has learned? I couldn't start screaming like Mikey, like a person with a disability — I simply do not have one. But I must confess that the urge to cry out and deny what I had learned was very strong.

*If anyone had told me a week before that there really **is** a God and that this God actually **gave** the Torah to the Jews (you and me) — a blueprint, so to speak, for how to live out our days on earth — I would have thought him insane. Yet here I sit, on an ordinary Monday morning, writing to you as one Jew to another, telling you that I am sure now that I have an important job to do here. I don't yet know the details of this job, but like any important job with a lot of responsibility, I know it won't be easy. Still, I feel certain it will be fulfilling.*

*Why am I telling **you** this? Because another memory I have from Nantasket Beach, maybe an even more potent image than that of poor Mikey, is my memory of the Orthodox Jews at the end of the street. Every day, I walked with my mother, sister and aunts to the beach. Sometimes it would be just two of us; other times we'd all go together. Our numbers were never consistent — but **you** were.*

All the information I ever had about you was contained in the sign on your front lawn which read: "Grand Rabbi Horowitz." There was something about that sign that I was sure would endure. It had such permanence. It was always there. When we would drive into Nantasket for the first weekend of the season, that sign was there to greet us, telling us we were almost home. And when I looked at that sign I always hoped that our house would be as enduring and would always provide the same sense of security and peace.

Whenever we passed by on our way to the beach, you were always at home, well-attended by your flock of family and followers. As a young girl of three, and five, and six and seven, I waved "hello" to all of you, sometimes repeatedly and enthusiastically. But there was never a response. You all had your heads buried in some books. Once in a while, a woman might lift her hand ever-so-slightly, and once a man nodded to my mother. When I asked her why you didn't wave back, my mother said it was probably forbidden in your religion.

But that didn't stop me. I continued to wave frantically to you for years. I wanted **contact***. I don't know why I should have wanted contact considering the fact that I was a little afraid of you, afraid of the way you dressed, the way you dressed the* **children***. Such hot clothes in the summer? And why did none of you ever go to the beach? You had that little wading pool in the yard for the kids, but still I pitied them. Their parents kept them imprisoned. Hot clothes and a hat in the middle of the summer and no beach or ice-cream man, only a rinky-dink plastic pool in the yard. And to top it all off, the guys had these long locks of hair coming down the sides of their heads! To a five-year-old, with all due respect, Rabbi, this looked like some strange and terrible kind of prison.*

Now, after my Jewish Discovery week, I am beginning to understand all these memories. My incessant waving that was never acknowledged, my fear of you, my feelings about your life style — all this turned me away from Judaism. (Not that there was ever anything Jewish in my life to turn away **from***. I guess I always knew, in a vague sort of way, that I was a Jew, but that had no meaning to me whatsoever.) I believe now that this was God's way of challenging me. You see, you made such an indelible impression on me; something in my life would never have been complete until I found out* **why** *— why I was so* *impressed and why you were the way you were. Everything else, all my other impressions of youth, were explained to me: Mikey was retarded. Doctors had determined that he was brain damaged and had the mentality of a three-year-old. That was why he behaved as he did. The complexities of your household, however, were never explained to me, not by anyone in my family or anyone else. No one checked it out, no one studied why you were the way you were. I signed up for the Discovery Program in order to find out.*

Little did I know that some genuine "heavyweights" lived down the block from me in Nantasket, people so committed to the Truth that they lived by God's word.

*I am no longer afraid when I see the tide rising — it's just a natural part of life; I am no longer afraid of Judaism — it's become a natural part of **my** life. I am no longer afraid of people like you, who dress and act strangely, because your clothing and behavior are not strange to me anymore.*

I realize now that my thoughts as a child about that sign on your lawn had a much deeper meaning. For all I know, the sign itself may by now have turned to dust, but what it represented was everlasting. I can see that sign very clearly now, standing there to greet me, telling me that I'm almost "home."

*It's sometimes hard to know the difference we make just by simply being ourselves, so I'm writing to let you know the **incredible** difference and the significant contribution you and your family have made to my life.*

God bless you, Rabbi. I will include you and your family in my prayers — when I learn from the Torah and from my teachers how and when to pray.

Take care and a hundred "Hello"s from your old neighbor and new partner,

Melissa Paine

Glossary

The following glossary provides a partial explanation of some of the Hebrew, Yiddish and Aramaic words and phrases used in this book. The spelling and explanations reflect the way the specific word is used in herein. Often, there are alternate spellings and meanings for the words.

ALIYAH: lit., ascent; immigration to ERETZ YISRAEL.

ARON KODESH: Holy Ark containing the Torah scrolls.

ASUR: forbidden by Jewish law.

BADECKEN: (Y.) part of the wedding ceremony, in which the groom covers the bride's face with a veil.

BARUCH DAYAN HA-EMES: "Blessed be the True Judge," a blessing recited upon hearing bad tidings.

BARUCH HASHEM: "Thank God!"

BAS BAYIS: a girl who is like one of the family.

BAS TORAH: an observant Jewish girl.

BAS YISRAEL: lit., a daughter of Israel, a Jewish girl.

BEDIKAS CHAMETZ: the search for leaven conducted on the night before PESACH.

BEIS (BATTEI) MIDRASH: house(s) of study.

BEN ZEKUNIM: a child born to parents in their old age.

BERACHAH: a blessing.

BITACHON: faith and trust in God.

CHALILAH: "Heaven forbid!"

CHALLAH: the portion of dough separated as the priest's share.

CHAMETZ: leavened foods that are prohibited during PESACH.

CHANUKAS HA-BAYIS: dedication ceremony.

CHAS V'SHALOM: "Heaven forbid!"

CHASSAN: a bridegroom.

CHASSID (CHASSIDIM): person(s) devoted to the service of God and ethical perfection.

CHASSIDUS: Chassidism, a religious and social movement founded by Rabbi Israel Baal Shem Tov in the 18th century.

CHEDER: (Y.) a religious primary school for boys.

CHESSED: lovingkindness.

CHEVRAH KADISHA: (A.) the burial society.

CHINNUCH: religious education.

CHOLOV YISROEL: milk, milked or supervised by a Jew.

CLOIZ: (Y.) a chassidic court.

CHUPPAH: the wedding canopy.

DAVEN: (Y.) to pray.

DAYAN: a judge in Torah law.

DAYENU: "It would have been sufficient" (orig., a refrain of a song from the Passover HAGGADAH).

DIN TORAH: a dispute judged by a rabbinical court.

EITZAH: advice.

ERETZ YISRAEL: the Land of Israel.

EZRAS NASHIM: the women's section in a synagogue.

FRUM: (Y.) religiously observant.

GABBAI: a secretary or treasurer of a synagogue.

GET: a bill of divorce according to Torah law.

GEULAH: the Redemption.

GEZUNTE BREN: (Y.) lit., a healthy fire; a fire from which heavy financial loss is sustained and no one is injured.

GLATT: (Y.) strictly (kosher).

HACHNASAS ORCHIM: hospitality.

HAGGADAH: the story of the Jews' redemption from Egypt, read during the SEDER on PESACH.

HALACHAH: Jewish law.

HAKADOSH BARUCH HU: The Holy One, Blessed Be He.

HANAVI: the prophet.

HASHEM: God.

HASHGACHAH PRATIS: Divine providence.

HAVDALAH: blessing recited at the end of Sabbaths and Festivals.

HOSHANAH RABBAH: the seventh day of SUKKOS.

INYAN: a subject; a matter.

KADDISH: the mourner's prayer.

KALLAH: a bride.

KASHRUS: the Jewish dietary laws.

KEDUSHAH: sanctity; holiness.

KEHILLAH: a Jewish community or congregation.

KELBENE-OIGEN: (Y.) lit., calves'-eyes, large expressive eyes imploring sympathy.

KENESSIAH GEDOLAH: a major convention.

KIDDUSH: sanctification of the Sabbath and Festivals, usually recited over a cup of wine.

KINDERLACH: (Y.) children.

KIPPAH: a skullcap.

KIRUV: bringing nonobservant Jews closer to Torah observance.

KLEZMER: (Y.) traditional Eastern European Jewish music.

KOLLEL: a center for advanced Torah learning for adult students, mostly married men.

KRECHTZ: (Y.) a sigh.

LAG B'OMER: the festive 33rd day of the 49-day mourning period between PESACH and Shavuos.

LANTSMAN: (Y.) one from the same village or country.

L'CHAIM: "To life," a toast.

LEVAYAH: a funeral.

MA'ARIV: the evening prayer service.

MAGGID: the narrative part of the HAGGADAH.

MATZOS: flat, unleavened bread eaten during PESACH.

MAZEL: (Y.) luck; fortune.

MAZEL UND BRACHA: (Y.) a blessing for the successful conclusion of a business deal.

MAYIM SHELANU: water for baking MATZOS which was drawn the day before and stored overnight.

MECHITZAH: the partition which separates the men's and women's sections in a synagogue.

MENUCHAH: rest.

MESHULACH (MESHULACHIM): lit., emissary(ries); fund-raiser(s).

MESIRUS NEFESH: dedication; self-sacrifice.

MIDDOS: good attributes.

MIDRASH: Homiletic teachings of the Sages.

MIKVEH: a ritual bath.

MINCHAH: the afternoon prayer service.

MINYAN (MINYANIM): ten adult male Jews, the minimum for congregational prayer.

MISHNAYOS: sections of the Mishnah, the primary basis of the Talmud.

MITZVAH (MITZVOS): Torah commandment(s); good deed(s).

MOETZES GEDOLEI HATORAH of ERETZ YISRAEL: the Council of Torah Sages of the Land of Israel.

NESHAMALEH: (Y.) a little soul.

NETILAS YADAYIM: the ritual washing of hands.

NIFTAR: deceased.

NIGGUNIM: (Chassidic) tunes or melodies.

NOSHES: (Y.) snacks.

OHEV YISRAEL: one who loves his fellow Jews.

PAYOS: sidelocks; long, usually curly sidelocks worn by CHASSIDIM.

PESACH: Passover.

PORITZ: a wealthy landowner.

POSEK: a halachic authority.

PURIM SHPIEL: a humorous skit performed on the holiday of Purim.

RABBOSAI: lit., my teachers; a respectful form of address.

RAV: a rabbi.

REB: (Y.) a respectful form of address.

REBBE: (Y.) a rabbi; a Torah teacher; a chassidic leader.

REBBETZIN: (Y.) the wife of a rabbi.

REFUAH SHELEMAH: "A complete recovery!"

RIBBONO SHEL OLAM: the Master of the Universe.

RISHON L'TZION: lit., the first in Zion, honorary title of the Sephardic
    Chief Rabbi.

ROSH CHODESH NISSAN: the first day of the month of Nissan.

ROSH YESHIVA: the dean of a YESHIVA.

SCHNORRERS: (Y.) beggars.

SEDER: PESACH night ceremony recalling the Exodus.

SEFER (SEFARIM): book(s); sacred book(s).

SEFER TOLDOS ADAM: one's life story.

SEFER TORAH: a Torah scroll.

SEUDAH: a festive meal.

SHABBATON: a weekend gathering for the purpose of KIRUV.

SHABBOS: the Sabbath.

SHABBOS HAGADOL: the Sabbath preceding PESACH.

SHACHARIS: the morning prayer service.

SHAILAH: (Y.) a halachic question.

SHALOM ALEICHEM: lit., "Peace be with you," a traditional greeting.

SHEMURAH MATZOS: MATZOS baked from wheat which has been
    "guarded" from becoming unleavened.

SHEVA BERACHOS: the seven benedictions recited at a wedding; one of
    the festive meals held in honor of the bride and groom during the
    week following the wedding, at which these blessings are said.

SHIDDUCH: a marital match.

SHIUR (SHIURIM): a Torah lesson(s).

SHLEPPING: (Y.). hauling.

SHLITA: acronym for "May he live long and happily, Amen!"

SHOCHET: a ritual slaughterer.

SHOFAR: a ram's horn, sounded in SHUL on the High Holy Days.

SHOMER: a guard or watchman.

SHOMER SHABBOS: a Sabbath-observer.

SHTADLANIM: intercessors.

SHTREIMLACH: (Y.) fur-trimmed hats worn by CHASSIDIM on festive occasions.

SHUL: (Y.) a synagogue.

SHULCHAN: a table.

SIFREI TORAH: Torah scrolls.

SIYATTA D'SHEMAYA: (A.) Heavenly assistance.

SUKKAH: a temporary booth for dwelling during SUKKOS.

SUKKOS: the Festival of Tabernacles.

TALMID CHACHAM: a scholar; a learned man.

TEFILLAH (TEFILLOS): prayer(s).

TEFILLAS HA-DERECH: a traveler's prayer for safety.

TEHILLIM: Psalms.

TISCH: (Y.) gathering of chassidim with their rebbe at a festive meal.

TREIF: (Y.) not kosher.

TZADDIK: a righteous, pious man; a holy man.

TZITZIS: a fringed garment.

UNTERFERER: (Y.) the groom's (or bride's) escort to the CHUPPAH.

UPSHAREN: (Y.) first-haircutting ceremony of a three-year-old boy.

YENNER and PLONY: (Y.) so and so.

YESHIVA: an academy of Torah study.

YICHUS: pedigree; distinguished lineage.

YIDDISHKEIT: (Y.) Judaism.

YINGELE: (Y.) a little boy.

YOM TOV: a Festival.

YUD: the tenth letter of the Hebrew alphabet.

ZECHER: a trace; remembrance.

Z"L: May his memory be a blessing.

ZT"L: May the memory of a righteous one be a blessing.